Rich and Tasty

Vermont Furniture to 1850

Rich and Tasty

Vermont Furniture to 1850

Jean M. Burks

Philip Zea

Shelburne Museum, Shelburne, Vermont
Distributed by University Press of New England

Foreword

Thomas Denenberg

REGIONALISM HAS SERVED AS THE ORGANIZING PRINCIPLE for scholarship in American furniture since the pioneering studies of the late nineteenth century. New England antiquarians gathered, sorted, and published the styles and types of their ancestors' worldly goods, invariably at the expense of a more ecumenical material record. In doing so, they created a canon of American furniture that initially prized historical association, but quickly came to be organized by aesthetics in the modern era. Interest in the oak, joined cradle that "rocked on the Mayflower" gave way to the connoisseurship of fashionable mahogany tables, chairs, and chests from Boston or Newport as collecting antiques became a popular avocation by the 1920s.

Geographic chauvinism held sway for decades. From the earliest published efforts of collectors such as Dr. Irving Lyon in the 1890s, through the entrepreneurial scholarship of Wallace Nutting, and into the mid-twentieth-century writings of Israel Sack, the cabinetmakers and shop traditions of coastal New England provided the archetypes against which all American furniture came to be measured (Philadelphia and New York provided worthy exceptions to prove the rule). In recent decades, new light has been cast into dark corners of the field as scholars investigated outlying areas within New England as well as the relationship of American furniture to the material culture of the Atlantic rim. Regions, it is now clear, are not hermetic. Ideas travel across the ocean, up river, and over mountains as surely as do people.

Then as now, Vermont—a state within a region—holds a special place in the American imagination. Mountainous, sparsely populated by taciturn Yankees, the Green Mountain State distills New England's role as the nation's attic—an idealized example of collective memory. It is the perfect microcosm for studying the creolization of furniture, the creation of a communal aesthetic that is unique, yet made up of influences from near and far. For years scholars and students have acknowledged that Vermont furniture "looks different." Is this motif adopted from New York? from Boston? Did the availability of exotic woods limit or liberate the craftsman? With *Rich and Tasty: Vermont Furniture to 1850* in hand, we now know the answers.

Exhibitions and their catalogues, like furniture, are the work of many hands. First and foremost, I would like to thank Jean Burks for recognizing the need for a scholarly reappraisal of Vermont furniture and for enlisting Phil Zea to the cause. Jean, Phil, and a group

of dedicated collectors organized this project in the grand spirit of collaboration and have given us an elegant book and exhibition.

J. David Bohl brought his unerring eye to the endeavor as photographer, a role he has played on countless studies of New England material culture. Jacquelyn Oak organized the images for this catalogue, but also kept the volume on track with grace and humor. Our catalogue team of Sandra Klimt, Margo Halverson, and Lucie Teegarden produced an elegant volume. It was a pleasure to once again work with Mike Burton and the staff at the University Press of New England. Institutional colleagues and individuals throughout New England responded time and time again to our requests for information, images, and loans. I would like to thank Rebecca Beall, Old Sturbridge Village; J. Brooks Buxton; Mark Hudson, Jacqueline Calder, Mary Rogstad, Vermont Historical Society; Daniel R. Davis; Prudence Doherty, Special Collections, University of Vermont; the Fowler Family; Mary and Norman Gronning; Philip Zea, Penny Leveritt, Historic Deerfield; Bernard and S. Dean Levy, Inc.; Marianne Martin, The Colonial Williamsburg Foundation; Duane Merrill; Ethan Merrill; Jim Orr, The Henry Ford; Jennie Shurtleff, Woodstock Historical Society; Robert Wolterstorff, Jamie Franklin, Callie Stewart, Bennington Museum; and Margaret Tamulonis, Fleming Museum, University of Vermont. At Shelburne Museum, Erin Barnaby, Sara Belisle, Nick Bonsall, Jim Brumsted, Jeff Bundy, Polly Darnell, Nicole DeSmet, Nancy Hileman, Kate Owen, Karen Petersen, Stephen Porter, Barbara Rathburn, Nancie Ravenel, Kory Rogers, and Suzanne Zaner all contributed to the success of the exhibition with characteristic enthusiasm and professionalism. We are especially grateful to the private collectors who have generously lent to the endeavor. We could not produce exhibitions and catalogues without the stalwart support of generous sponsors such as The Americana Foundation and longtime museum friend Brooks Buxton. I would also like to acknowledge the unflagging support of the board of trustees of Shelburne Museum for their support of scholarly exhibitions such as *Rich and Tasty*.

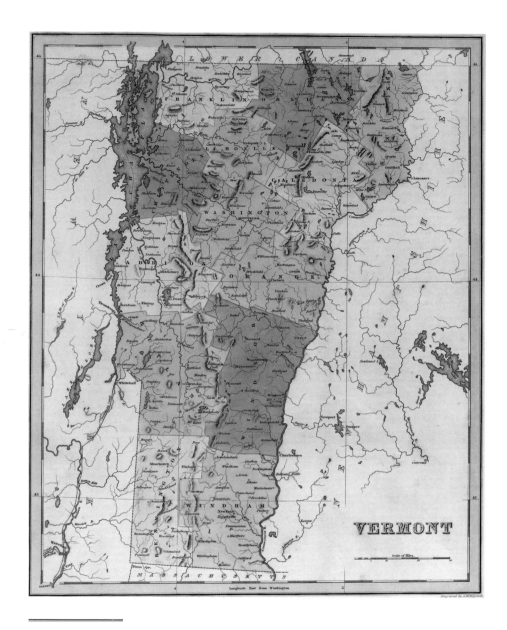

FIGURE 1

Map of Vermont, 1838

Entered according to Act of Congress in the year 1838, by T. G. Bradford,
in the Clerk's Office, of the District Court of Massachusetts

Fleming Museum of Art, University of Vermont

A Primer for Light Grade Amber and Pure Vermont Furniture

Philip Zea

IN THE TUESDAY, JUNE 2, 1829, EDITION of the *Vermont Gazette*, Bennington cabinetmaker Hastings Kendrick (born 1804) reported his move from nearby Shaftsbury to "the shop on Main-street . . . where he intends to manufacture a variety of rich and tasty FURNITURE from the best materials and in the best manner . . . [and that] he intends to keep on hand, and to manufacture, all kinds of Furniture usually found in a Cabinet Warehouse, as cheap as can be afforded. All kinds of CARVING done on short notice."[1] Kendrick had left the countryside for a central location on Main Street where his knowledge of current style and access to fine lumber and hardware would support the manufacture and sale of *his own* stockpiled furniture which also might highlight his specialized skill as a carver.

Kendrick was balancing the attractions of modern salesmanship with the heritage of traditional furniture-making, in which a chest or a desk was commissioned by the customer rather than purchased from stockpiled goods made by a variety of craftsmen. With a dash of his pen, Kendrick captured the complexity of Vermont's economy and the demand for stylish household goods at a time when prosperity was interwoven with merino sheep, cast-iron stove foundries, and marble quarries. The results, like the half-sideboard or "locker" (in Vermont terminology) that bears Kendrick's initials and a date four years earlier than the advertisement, capture a range of skills keyed to the specific culture and economy of Vermont (Fig. 2).

The integrity of Kendrick's design and execution seems at odds, or just odd, when aligned with our modern *beliefs* about Vermont, Vermonters, and their various characteristics. Kendrick's controlled architecture, inventive design, and skillful merger of superior materials

seem inconsistent with today's salient images from the Vermont Department of Tourism, of Ethan Allen, ski trails, Jersey cows, and Ben & Jerry's ice cream. The fact that these are valid twenty-first-century impressions, buoyed by folklore about rock-ribbed independence and frugality, underscores that the bucolic can be complicated and that choice and change come to the fore after other alternatives wear out.

Unearthing the *real* material culture of the Green Mountain State rather than modern impressions of it, or questioning that it even existed given the grinding millstones of poverty and peculiarity, has been a fifty-year process to date. The gauntlet was thrown down by Charles Montgomery in his 1966 book *American Furniture of the Federal Period*, where he stated that the ambitious bombé bureau at the Winterthur Museum signed "Made by G. Stedman Norwich VT" (see Cat. 20) was "a bizarre conception" built by a craftsman "about whom nothing is known"—almost as if it were impossible to find Stedman or perhaps not even worth trying; that is, until David Hewitt did precisely that twenty years later in the 1980s.[2] Bill Hosley's research and writing in the 1970s and 1980s focused on defining the sophisticated cultural and economic setting that explains why inventive architecture, gravestones, and furniture like Stedman's *are* plausible for Vermont two or three generations after settlement in the 1760s. Hosley joined Nancy Graff and others in 1991 to celebrate the bicentennial of Vermont's statehood by comparing Vermont myths and realities in order to improve how we see Vermont's heritage. Then in the 1990s, I teamed up with Charles Robinson and Ken Zogry on separate projects with Shelburne Museum and the Bennington Museum to document as many craftsmen and objects as possible in order to imagine the breadth and complexity of Vermont furniture-making statewide as an interpretive whole.

Now, two decades later, Jean Burks of Shelburne Museum asks what have we learned, and unlearned, about Vermont furniture during the last twenty years. Why does furniture made in the Old Republic seem somehow more closely aligned on a statewide basis with the environment that produced it than does regional furniture made and owned in other parts of the country? Our current quest to understand Vermont through its furniture, and vice versa, takes the form of defining the qualities and characteristics of the furniture itself. Spurred to action by the discovery of several documented examples of Vermont furniture over the last two decades, many of which are illustrated for the first time in this book, we now know about the work of many more craftsmen and see that their work sharpens our understanding of the material legacy of Vermont.

From the perspective of history, part of the answer is that *our* Vermont was not *their* Vermont, which was settled after the French and Indian War in the 1760s. The pressure for fertile land, even along the steep valleys of Vermont, created a flood of resettlement from southern New England and an investment boom that could not wait to develop for profit every mill and farm that might be had. Adding to the pressure were factors including the politics and inflationary economy after the American Revolution and conflicting land grants in Vermont chartered by both New Hampshire and New York. In this setting Vermonters took a proactive stand and created an independent republic that lasted from 1777 until 1791, when Vermont became the fourteenth state. From that point, between 1790 and 1810, the state's population grew 150 percent. Everything was rosy—even cutting edge—until Jefferson's Embargo of 1807, the War of 1812, and the resulting post-war collapse of the economy ended Vermont's halcyon era with depression. But in a very Vermont-like way, two important events occurred: Jefferson's consul to Portugal, William Jarvis (1770–1859) of Weathersfield, Vermont, smuggled out of Spain an exotic herd of merino sheep that he brought home to the Connecticut valley in 1811. These sheep created the basis of the next boom economy. Second, some Vermonters in the Champlain and Connecticut valleys perfected their own skills as smugglers via British Canada, bypassing the President's embargo. Buoyed again by natural resources, in Vermont's very earth, the marble and then the iron foundry industries had their prosperous beginnings.

This Vermont, of the 1780s to the 1840s, forged the cauldron of ambition and imagination that created the bulk of Vermont furniture that we love today. Then, it ended. No other than Horace Greeley (1811–72), who had apprenticed to a printer in East Poultney as a fifteen-year-old, and who eventually became the editor of the *New York Tribune* and Democratic candidate for the presidency in 1872, advised all young men after the Panic of 1837 to "go to the Great West, anything rather than to stay here."[3] Most of those who left were anonymous, but not all—for example, Stephen A. Douglas (1813–61) of Brandon, who trained as a cabinetmaker with Nahum Parker of Middlebury and later with Caleb Knowlton in Brandon and vied with Lincoln for the presidency in 1860.[4]

Why did they leave? The opening of the Erie Canal system after the mid-1820s first drew the ambitious away from the worn hill towns of Vermont to the promise of rock-free farms and an expanding population in the West. To this day, native Vermonters lamenting a neighbor's death will say that the deceased "went west." Still, by 1860 the Census of Manufactures recorded 150 cabinetmakers, 50 chairmakers, and 75 bedstead manufacturers in Vermont, many placed on the landscape near waterpower and a center of population.[5] The following year brought the great national calamity, the American Civil War, which briefly revived the wool industry but cropped the promise of the entire next generation in the ranks of the two Vermont brigades whose sacrifice brought the Green Mountain State the Union's second highest percentage of per capita casualties while over a tenth of the population was in uniform.[6]

FIGURE 2
Half Sideboard, dated October 7, 1825
Attributed to Jonathan Hastings Kendrick (b. 1804)
Shaftsbury, Vermont
Mahogany, mahogany veneer, and eastern white pine
H. 58 ½ x W. 49 ¾ x D. 23 ¼ inches
The Bennington Museum

The printed words of Kendrick, Greeley, and Douglas easily capture the mood of their generations as a cultural statement. The furniture and other household goods that they grew up with and owned (and in Kendrick's and Douglas's cases could build) better illustrate the actual conditions in which they lived. The concept of consumerism, which begins on a regional basis, links economics and taste. As with all furniture and other household goods, there is a language and vocabulary that surrounds the physical evidence of manufacture and use which in this instance is applied to understanding Vermont furniture on its own terms. This kind of connoisseurship is tested in twelve inquiries defined as Design, Precedent, Materials, Craftsmanship, Workmanship, Ornamentation, Innovation, Technology, Rarity, Originality, Condition, and Provenance.[7]

Our primer for understanding these wooden slivers of Vermont culture begins with **Design**: the craftsman's plan for combining practical functions with some semblance of proportion and acceptable taste. For example, chairs are particularly difficult to design because they must support an active sitter who may wish to move the chair from room to room. Chairs must evoke confidence, look inviting, and elevate the social aspects of one's presumed place at the table or in the parlor. Chairs also must be comfortable, and by their nature they are low in height, so beauty must be found in looking down at them rather than up. The rocking, comb-back Windsor armchair epitomizes successful chair design by embracing all of these concerns (see Cat. 10 and 13). Furthermore, successful Windsor chairs are constructed from a variety of woods with different properties and appearances, which are then stained or painted to unify the design. Most of their parts are attached to the central plank or seat, allowing them to flex like a suspension bridge in order to accommodate both the most corpulent and delicate of Vermonters. This classic expression of seating engineering also rocks back and forth, tempting calamity with moving weight, while the head is comforted and perfectly framed by the crown-like "comb."[8]

The second category is **Precedent**, where we find that nothing is new under the sun in the realm of consumer goods and that ideas for design and construction almost always have roots. For example, the bombé-facade furniture by George Stedman was inspired by French furniture designs, rather than English, in all likelihood because during most of the Napoleonic Wars the French were American allies and the English were not; politics more than culture inspired Stedman and his patrons. By the same token, many early neoclassical card tables from both eastern and western Vermont have five legs, like New York card tables, because New York City for a time was both the seat of the Federal government and the economic capital of the new nation (see Cat. 21, Samuel Stow card table, and Cat. 24, western Vermont card table). Furthermore, one-sixth of Vermont lies in the watershed of the Hudson River, which facilitated commerce and exchange of ideas. Those families who held land grants from New York may have felt: *the more legs the better!* By the same token, some case furniture made in the Middlebury area of western Vermont holds an affinity with Essex County, Massachusetts, and coastal New Hampshire designs because important craftsmen moved to Addison County, Vermont, from northeast of Boston (see Cat. 35, Shelburne Museum Bureau). That coincides with knowing that 54 percent of the furniture craftsmen who emigrated to Vermont before 1825 were from Massachusetts (34 percent) and New Hampshire (20 percent), while another 27 percent were native Vermonters.[9]

Materials compose the third category. The raw materials found (or not found) in an object reflect the economy in which it was made as well as the status of the patron. Consequently, documentation to a place is just as important as documentation to the maker and first owner. Critical to this economic equation is the fact that each piece of furniture is a microcosm of context—a kind of snapshot taken when it was made or perhaps later altered—and that it is also built of materials other than wood—such as glass, cloth, hardware and other metal fasteners, and that it may have finishes such as stain, paint, and varnish, each of which came from somewhere near or far. The closer materials are often expedient and cheap while the distant ones are more exotic and expensive and therefore connote status. Together they tell us the economic worldview of the first owner and maker.

Vermont furniture is a bit different in this regard because it often entails visually exotic materials that *are* native, like vibrant bird's-eye maple, as well as imports from an ocean away, like mahogany. The governing principle, as with early neoclassical urban furniture from the New England seacoast, is based on the concept of flat surfaces manipulated by contrasting veneers. Where urban furniture, especially northeast of Boston, might feature sheets of dark mahogany contrasted with imported satinwood veneer on the very best examples or with vibrant birch on somewhat lesser furniture, Vermont cabinet-makers, particularly those west of the Green Mountains, inverted the idea, employing their graphic maple veneers contrasted with sparingly used, expensive mahogany. Consequently, the discerning connoisseur of Vermont furniture sees in the case furniture made in the Champlain Valley a graphic composition of contrasting veneers, usually local maple and imported mahogany, materials that result in furniture of surprising brightness. The furniture, while quirky in its uniqueness, is nevertheless a tour de force (see Cat. 54–57, western Vermont bureaus).

Vermonters, both craftsmen and consumers, knew and extolled the material wealth and natural beauty of the Green Mountain State despite its challenging weather. Zadock Thompson (1796–1856), in his encyclopedic *History of Vermont, Natural, Civil, and Statistical* (1842), catalogued the flora and fauna of Vermont for both its identification *and* inspiring qualities. When he came to woods used in furniture, Thompson wrote about the sugar maple (*Acer saccharinum*) that:

> When thoroughly seasoned ["rock maple"] is used by wheelwrights for axletrees and by sleigh makers for the runners of common sleds. It is also used by chair makers and cabinet makers in many kinds of their work. The wood of this tree exhibits

two accidental forms of arrangement of the fibre, of which cabinet makers take advantage for manufacturing beautiful articles of furniture. The first consists of undulations, forming what is called *Curled Maple* ["striped" or "tiger"]. The second, which occurs only in old trees, appears to arise from an inflection of the fibre from the circumference towards the centre, producing spots, which are sometimes continuous, and at others a little distance apart. This is what is called *Bird's-Eye Maple*, and the more numerous the spots, the more beautiful and more esteemed is the wood. Like curled and striped maple, it is used for inlaying mahogany. It is also made into bedsteads, portable writing desks, and a variety of other articles. . . . The sugar maple is the most valuable wood for fuel found in the state. . . . Its wood may easily be distinguished from other kinds of maple by its weight and hardness. Valuable as this tree is on account of its wood, and for being one of our most beautiful and flourishing ornamental shade trees, its value is greatly increased on account of the sugar extracted from it. . . . The quantity of sugar manufactured in the state in 1840 was 4,647,934 lbs.[10]

Other native woods were used in furniture (and implements) because of particular molecular advantages and their appearance. Black cherry (*Cerasus serotina*), which in Vermont was also called "cabinet cherry" and when stained takes on the appearance of mahogany, "is compact, fined [sic] grained, brilliant, and not liable to warp [unlike yellow birch] when perfectly seasoned. It is extensively used for almost all species of furniture and sometimes rivals mahogany in beauty, but it has been sought for with so much eagerness, that there is very little now remaining in our forests large enough to be sawn into boards."[11]

Thompson continues with his descriptions of Vermont trees, always pausing for more interpretation when they are found in furniture: red or "swamp" maple (*Acer rubrum*) for its beauty and ease of turning on a lathe; white ash (*Fraxinus acuminata*), especially in

FIGURE 3
Sofa (1826–31)
Attributed to the workshops of John B. Warner (1806–63)
Wallingford and Manchester, Vermont
Mahogany, mahogany veneer, cherry, maple, and eastern white pine
H. 84 x W. 88 x D. 21 inches
The Bennington Museum

common chairs for its "strength and elasticity"; yellow birch (*Betula excelsa*) for its broad diameter and versatility which "the cabinetmaker [uses] for bedsteads, tables, and numerous other articles of household furniture"; and sycamore (*Platanus occidentalis*) which "is little used by cabinet makers, in the form of boards, on account of its liability to warp, but it answers well for bedsteads, and requires only to be polished and varnished, without paint, to make a very neat article."[12] For the common secondary woods in Vermont furniture, Thompson of course notes the white pine (*Pinus strobus*) for its size but notes that by the 1840s, like cherry, it had been over-harvested and was difficult to obtain. More common as a secondary wood in Vermont furniture after 1820 is lightweight and aromatic basswood (*Tilia americana*), about which Thompson only reports that it is "valuable for very many purposes [including] planks and boards, and is used for chair seats, trunks, and in the manufacture of a variety of other articles."[13]

All of these woods and others were employed by Vermont cabinetmakers to great effect. When St. Albans cabinetmaker Lewis Beals (ca. 1780–1829) died in August 1829, his probate inventory listed over one hundred hand tools, unfinished stock in trade, and "400 ft. bass boards, 100 ft. curley [*sic*] maple, 90 ft refuse butternut [white walnut], refuse cherry boards... [and] 3 pieces of mahogany," just what Beals needed in proportion to build his opulent sideboard—whereabouts still unknown—which remains vibrant even in the black-and-white photograph published in 1970 in *The Magazine Antiques*.[14] By the same token, the account book of Nathan Burnell (1790–1860) of Swanton and Milton records his acquisition of *thousands* of board feet of lumber of various species, which in 1825 alone included: cherry (415, 334½, and 219 feet); maple (50, 104, and 108 feet) ; butternut (6,000, 754, 432, 217, 116, and 113 feet); walnut (one board 95 feet); birch (259 feet) and curly birch (74 feet).[15] Burnell's commercial activity underscores the fact that many of these craftsmen, while remembered as furniture makers, were also lumber merchants.

Since Vermont cabinetmakers invested both in Caribbean mahogany and in time making native woods appear like mahogany, the questions arise: How did they obtain it? In what form? And at what expense? Nahum Parker (1789–1876) was a cabinetmaker in Middlebury (and one of Stephen A. Douglas's masters; see Cat. 39, Nahum Parker sofa). Among Parker's papers is an 1828 receipt for highly specialized, expensive lumber purchased in Boston from Benjamin Lamson in both planks (thickness greater than two inches) and boards. Some of it—true mahogany *Swietenia mahagoni*—was shipped principally from Santo Domingo and Cuba. Parker also purchased "Bay Branch" boards, or Honduran mahogany *Swietenia macrophylla*, which is blonder in color and was harvested on the mainland of Central America in the vicinity of the Bay of Campeche.

Mr. Nahum Parker Bot of Benj. Lamson Boston Oct 1st 1828	
one St. domingo Mahogany Plank	$3.08
one St. domingo 1 ¼" Mahogany Plank	1.25
two St. domingo Mahogany Boards—13 ft. each—at 1/ pr ft	4.33
Five St. domingo Mahogany Boards 34 ft at 1/	5.67
Four St domingo Mahogany Boards 40 ft at 20 cts	9.60
Two Bay Branch Boards at $1.60 cts each	3.36
One Bay Branch Board 13 ft at 1/5 per ft.	3.25
	30.54
3 board at	3.25
One St Domino Plank at	4.68
Amt[?] Recpt	$38.47

227 feet transport 5.00   2 cts or foot[16]

Just as significantly, Parker did not deal exclusively with Boston merchants, nor did he incorporate in his furniture ornamental components only of his making. Filed with the previous bill in his papers is another, dated October 23, 1830, from D. L. Brower, Mahogany Yard, 186 Chambers Street, New York, where Parker ordered for $14.25: "2 Setts of Pillar & Claws Carved @ $7.00," which presumably were made of mahogany. Similarly there are two more bills totaling a whopping $98.72, on April 25, 1840, and June 20, 1844, with the firm of Ash & Thorp on Pearl Street in New York, which supplied Parker with imported tools, upholstery material, and an extensive list of brass and iron fittings and fasteners of various sorts.[17] Surprisingly, perhaps, some furniture from Vermont's "back of beyond" was made of Caribbean and English imports shaped partly by craftsmen in Boston and New York!

Craftsmanship comes next: the trained ability to master materials and to merge them in order to achieve design and visual impact. Imagine here that you are a young competitor of cabinetmaker Nathan Burnell of Milton about the time, 1850, when he was sixty years old and a well-established craftsman. Through your shop door comes a banker or the headmaster of an academy—someone seeking a stylish table for a set number of people. You reply of course that you make fine furniture from superior materials and in the latest Empire styles. Then your potential patron says, "Wonderful! Can you make for me a center table of the most beautiful, hard maple that you can find for . . . eleven people?" You reply, "An eleven-sided table?" And then to yourself, "Eleven is a prime number. How *will* I make it equi-sided out of the hardest wood found in Vermont and how on earth will I cut and match all of those angled joints in the table frame?" A few weeks later, up the street, old Nathan Burnell makes the table for your client not long before your move west to Iowa! (See Cat. 67, Burnell Center Table.)

Then we have **Workmanship**, the ability to work quickly and efficiently over long hours in order to make a living. All the God-given craftsmanship in the universe, often seen in the eye and hand of an accomplished artist, will not put bread on the table unless "the tricks of the trade" are applied to another old adage: "time is money." In reality there are three kinds of workmanship: certainty, risk, and economics. David Pye wrote about the first two in a book titled *The Nature and Art of Workmanship* (1968).[18] Pye describes first the "Workmanship of Certainty," wherein knowledge of the properties of tools and how to use them predicts accuracy in efficient ways. In other words, measuring devices, templates, and jigs shape wood (or any material) in such a way that the finished work appears precise and effortless, like the profile of a bracket foot drawn first with the help of a template. By the same token, the "Workmanship of Risk" rests with eye-hand coordination and little mechanical guidance. Chisels and gouges, for example, are the principal tools of the carver, whose work in wood is the epitome of the workmanship of risk. One slip of the wrist and an entire morning's work may be lost. The Workmanship of Risk provides the tension and excitement that often leads to the impression of beauty.

Lastly, there is a third kind of workmanship, the "Workmanship of Economics," wherein the economy in which the craftsman works must be large and prosperous enough to provide the craftsman with quality tools and materials as well as sufficient regular demand for his work to allow him to make a living and to provide a platform for repetitive perfection and the development of new ideas. The highest inherent craftsmanship will wither from lack of use if patrons, tools, and materials are unavailable. By example, perhaps for lack of repetition, John B. Warner (1806–63) of Wallingford and Manchester (his shops operated simultaneously) apparently had no way to improve his modest carving skills nor experience to devise a system to support his sofa frame with fashionable saber legs, which instead are supplanted by functional front legs behind the stylish ones (Fig. 3). Each kind of workmanship embraces knowledge, materials, and tools. The latter conveys just how sophisticated and demanding craftsmanship can be. If you study the surviving, complete tool chest of Nathan Burnell, you will never think again that the ability to make this furniture required anything less than professional expertise.[19]

Ornamentation follows next: decorative detail that is usually current and derived from expensive materials and/or the Workmanship of Risk. Ornamentation is the icing on the cake. Whether found in the wonderful inlaid swags on the friezes of the case furniture by Rufus Norton (1783–1818) from Windsor (see Cat. 18 and 19), or the ornamental painted scenes by Charles Curtis (1801–76) on the twelve director's chairs made for the Bank of Burlington about 1822 (see Cat. 8), the devil is in the details. For example, consider just a section of the secretary bookcase made by Hastings Warren (1779–1845) in Middlebury about 1830 (see Fig. 4). First there is Warren's design, which thematically applies principles of classical architecture to furniture. Then we have the contrasting light native veneer of maple against the imported mahogany veneers, which here are seen manipulated in every way there is: molded and sawn on the muntins of the glazed door, flat and cross-banded in the door frame and frieze of the cornice, and turned and carved in the Ionic capital of the column, which itself is a tapering, mahogany-veneered cylinder—all implemented in this detail only a foot square.

Furniture ornament in Vermont further embraces the idea that more is better, as found on this dressing table from the Champlain Valley with multiple contrasting veneers spread out over torus-molded and flat drawer facades, its overhanging case, and shaped backboard (Fig. 6). The design is crowded with ornament, including a pair of applied, turned drops. The implementation of the design was costly and probably came close to matching the expense of a full-sized bureau. The same may be true of the Bugbee family drop-leaf table from Pomfret, near Woodstock (Fig. 5). Sometimes Vermont ornamentation simply takes the form of exaggeration or even simply of repetition. In this case, if four or six legs are perfect for a dining table, then eight are even better, increasing the table's cost and making it nearly impossible to seat company for dinner!

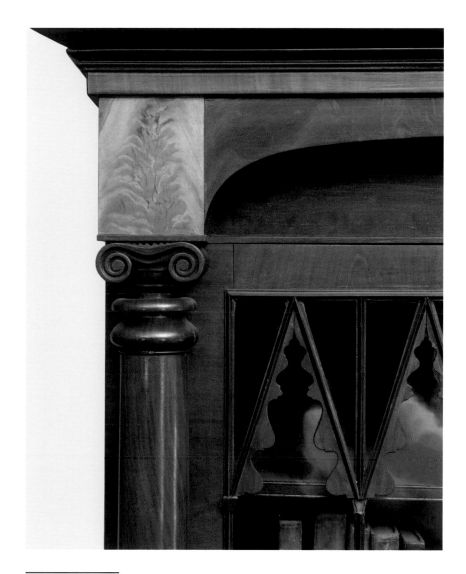

FIGURE 4
Detail, Secretary, ca. 1830
Attributed to workshop of Hastings Warren (1779–1845)
Middlebury, Vermont
Mahogany, cherry, mahogany and birch veneers, and eastern white pine
H. 92 ½ x W. 55 x D. 23 inches
Sheldon Museum

FIGURE 5
Drop-Leaf Table, ca. 1825
Pomfret-Woodstock, Vermont, area
Cherry and yellow birch
H. 27 ¾ x W. 48 x D. 46 ½ inches
Historic Deerfield, Inc., 1989.047
Gift of F. Earl Williams in memory of Dr. N. P. Bugbee

FIGURE 6
Dressing Table, ca. 1830
Champlain Valley, perhaps Burlington, Vermont
Cherry, maple, maple and mahogany veneers, and basswood
H. 39 ½ x W. 26 ¾ x D. 19 ¾ inches
Author's Collection

7/2386636

Here is **Innovation**: the state of finding something new under the sun against all odds in design, technology, craftsmanship, ornamentation, and/or materials. Within this realm, there are two kinds of innovation: good and bad, in either case always inspiring. First, for example, is the development of a new regional form, the half sideboard or locker, that incorporates the templates of a bureau into a foreshortened sideboard to economize space in the small, low-posted houses of Vermont built before 1830 (see Cat. 40, 41, and 42). Or consider the two cradles from Brandon and Barnet (see Cat. 1 and 2). Who says that furniture must be constructed of wood? And who says that cradles must rock side to side? The prize for innovation in Vermont furniture design, however, goes to James Richardson (1794–1861) of Poultney for his worktable or writing desk, which is constructed of numerous native woods for strength, lightness, and contrast (see Cat. 46). This table answers the functional needs for mobility by being lightweight and accessible for storage and for the sitter. The table bears a work surface that is stable and strong, despite the appearance of top-heaviness, while its endless curves delight the eye with a nod to classicism through the four columns and saber legs.

Then there is **Rarity**: the condition of being unique, or nearly so, without necessarily the connotation of costliness. Glossy auction catalogs and magazines are peppered with numerous treasures all labeled as rare or (my favorite) "very rare." One wonders just how rare "rare" is. Are Boston block-front chests and desks at all rare? Rare is one of the finest clocks available in America at the time: the girandole clock or "parlour timepiece" made in Burlington in 1821 by Lemuel Curtis (1790–1857) and Joseph Nye Dunning (1795–1841), with the painted tablet depicting the story of Daniel attributed to Charles Curtis (Fig. 7). The survival of the printed instructions (Fig. 8), published in Burlington, proves that Curtis made his elaborate wall clock design, patented in 1816 in direct competition with the Simon and Aaron Willard's models, in Vermont after leaving home in Concord, Massachusetts. Proof of its Vermont origins are further substantiated by the thermometer mounted in the waist of the case which records parlor weather to forty degrees below zero.

Originality in the survival of all parts, fasteners, and surface treatments from the time of construction in excellent **Condition** with no damage or alterations is epitomized by the ca. 1800 high chest of drawers that descended in the intermarried Dutton and Metcalf families of Norwich (see Cat. 6). Every aspect of this high chest of drawers survives unaltered from the day it was delivered by the cabinetmaker in Norwich or Hanover, New Hampshire, to the Dutton House on Dutton Road atop Dutton Hill. The high chest survives as such because it literally did not move until Shelburne Museum purchased it at auction in 1990.

That leaves us with **Provenance**: documented knowledge of who made the object and who has owned it down to the present time. Provenance is the gateway to context and to understanding what has influenced the uses and meanings of the object. Context is the most important tool of connoisseurship, and the one least used. If you understand both the physical qualities of an artifact and the context in which it was made and owned, you can say with greater certainty how the object has been treated and perceived, making it more relevant as a true cultural statement.

In the world of Vermont furniture, the Dutton-Metcalf high chest of drawers is a good example of the importance of a complete provenance. Another is the wonderful neoclassical washstand made by Horace Nichols (1788–1849) in Middlebury in 1820 (see Cat. 30). We know that because it is inscribed in graphite with identification of the cabinetmaker and the three generations of owners down to the last. Such documentation is critical to fully enjoying a topic like Vermont furniture because we can place objects on the landscape. Want to feel good about yourself? Take a good Number 2 pencil and make the next generation of curators and collectors happy by writing *on* your furniture; labels and index cards will not do.

FIGURE 7

Girandole Wall Clock, ca. 1821

Made by Lemuel Curtis (1790–1857) and Joseph Nye Dunning (1795–1841)

Églomisé painting attributed to Charles Curtis (1801–1876)

Burlington, Vermont

Gilded and painted eastern white pine

H. 45 x W. 12 x D. 5 inches (7 including the eagle)

Collection of Bernard and S. Dean Levy, Inc.

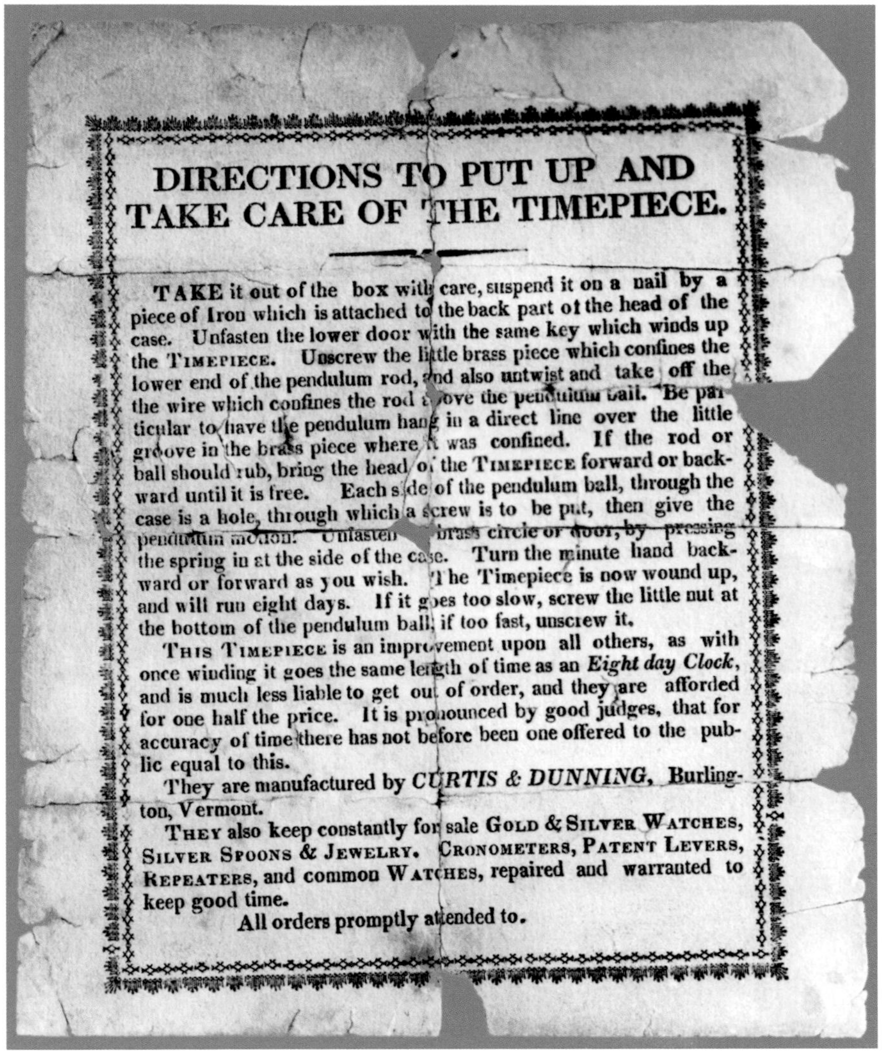

DIRECTIONS TO PUT UP AND TAKE CARE OF THE TIMEPIECE.

TAKE it out of the box with care, suspend it on a nail by a piece of Iron which is attached to the back part of the head of the case. Unfasten the lower door with the same key which winds up the TIMEPIECE. Unscrew the little brass piece which confines the lower end of the pendulum rod, and also untwist and take off the the wire which confines the rod above the pendulum ball. Be particular to have the pendulum hang in a direct line over the little groove in the brass piece where it was confined. If the rod or ball should rub, bring the head of the TIMEPIECE forward or backward until it is free. Each side of the pendulum ball, through the case is a hole, through which a screw is to be put, then give the pendulum motion. Unfasten brass circle or door, by pressing the spring in at the side of the case. Turn the minute hand backward or forward as you wish. The Timepiece is now wound up, and will run eight days. If it goes too slow, screw the little nut at the bottom of the pendulum ball; if too fast, unscrew it.

THIS TIMEPIECE is an improvement upon all others, as with once winding it goes the same length of time as an *Eight day Clock*, and is much less liable to get out of order, and they are afforded for one half the price. It is pronounced by good judges, that for accuracy of time there has not before been one offered to the public equal to this.

They are manufactured by CURTIS & DUNNING, Burlington, Vermont.

THEY also keep constantly for sale GOLD & SILVER WATCHES, SILVER SPOONS & JEWELRY. CRONOMETERS, PATENT LEVERS, REPEATERS, and common WATCHES, repaired and warranted to keep good time.

All orders promptly attended to.

FIGURE 8
Printed Instructions for Girandole Wall Clock, ca. 1821
H. 8 x W. 6 inches
Collection of Bernard and S. Dean Levy, Inc.

FIGURE 9
Server, ca. 1825
Stenciled: "Wm. Wilmot, cabinetmaker, Unadilla N.Y."
Unadilla, New York
Cherry, maple and mahogany veneers, and eastern white pine
H. 41 x W. 37 x D. 31 ¼ inches
New York State Museum

This high level of documentation would remove the final, disturbing variable from the study of Vermont furniture, which is that not all *Vermont-looking* furniture is from Vermont! It is from upstate New York, which was settled by thousands of expatriate New Englanders whose aesthetics, skill sets, and access to materials were identical to those of their cousins left behind. To this day as one travels westward through New York along Routes 5, 9, 17, 20 and so on into towns that, like Vermont, have fabulous nineteenth-century architecture, one asks: Where are all of the household goods that furnished these villas and temples nearly two centuries ago? Surprisingly little survives with documentation, but some looks as if it came from Vermont, begging the point that many anonymous objects sold or collected as from Vermont are not. (See further discussion of this topic in the "Three Vermont Furniture Puzzles" section of this book, pp. 120–137.)

One example is the server (Fig. 9), probably from the 1820s, stenciled "Wm. Wilmot, cabinetmaker, Unadilla, N.Y.," which is in Otsego County in south-central New York State. Wilmot apparently had no ties to Vermont. He was born in 1790 in Danbury, Connecticut, and as a young man moved to Unadilla, where he became the town's first cabinetmaker, remaining there until his death in 1849. The server, with wonderful contrasting veneers and an exaggerated splashboard that scream Vermont, is made of cherry, maple, and white pine with bird's-eye maple and mahogany veneers—exactly what you would expect— right down to the spiral-turned legs.[20] But it is not a Vermonter.

The study of Vermont furniture remains a work in process. Close examination of each newly discovered example reveals surprising craftsmanship and the impact of use and abuse over time. We usually assume that change is unplanned and often relatively recent, but proving that change was good even among staid Vermonters, there is the timeless 1856 letter written by Cynthia Goodrich to her cabinetmaker brother, Norman Jones (1790–1874), back home in Hubbardton:

Middlebury. Dear Brother. I will just write a line concerning my things which are at Hubbardton. I would like to have you varnish my Beuro and table which is at the Whipple house and Bedstead at Edward's, and those dining Chairs which were at Mother's, I would like to have painted over if you think they are worth it. The Great-Chair I would like to have made a little lower if it can be done without much Trouble. I would like to have new Trimmings [brasses] for my Beuro the kind you think most suitable. . . . We shall probably visit you in two or three weeks or as soon as the going is good and would like to have the things ready. Will you please write what the expense would be of carrying them to the nearest Rail Road station and if a team [of horses] could be procured.[21]

We cannot know whether Cynthia Goodrich left a trail of exasperation wherever she went, but we do know that like most consumers she wanted things to appear shiny and new and whenever possible modern, and she wanted things, particularly old ones, to feel comfortable at the very least. She knew where to find specialists and how to gain their attention. And like us today, Cynthia was in a rush and willing to bear the expense of shipping overnight even by railroad then a decade old. When aspects of the human condition are combined with an understanding of their social and cultural contexts, our "primer" for learning about a place through its things allows the chance for deeper appreciation of our surroundings and of those who have gone before. That is why to this day, per the 1829 advertisement of Hastings Kendrick, we seek "rich and tasty FURNITURE" that makes us smile.

1. *Vermont Gazette*, Tuesday, June 2, 1829.

2. Charles F. Montgomery, *American Furniture: The Federal Period,* (New York: Viking Press, 1966), 189-190; David Hewett, "G. Stedman—The Elusive Vermont Cabinetmaker," *Maine Antiques Digest* 14, no. 3 (March 1986): 1D-4D; William N. Hosley, Jr., "Architecture and Society of the Urban Frontier: Windsor, Vermont, in 1800," Peter Benes, ed. *The Bay and the River: 1600–1900. Annual Proceedings of the Dublin Seminar for New England Folklife* 6 (1981): 73–86; William N. Hosley, Jr., "Vermont Furniture, 1790–1830," in *New England Furniture: Essays in Memory of Benno Forman*, Brock Jobe, ed. (Boston: Society for the Preservation of New England Antiquities, 1987); *Old-Time New England* 72, no. 259 (1987): 245–86; William N. Hosley, Jr. and Nancy Price Graff, "Celebrating Vermont: Myths and Realities of the First Sixty Years of Statehood," in Richard H. Saunders and Virginia M. Westbrook, *Celebrating Vermont: Myths and Realities* (Middlebury, VT: Middlebury College, 1991), 19–43; Philip Zea, "Craftsmen and Culture: An Introduction to Vermont Furniture Making," in Charles A. Robinson, *Vermont Cabinetmakers & Chairmakers before 1855* (Shelburne, VT: Shelburne Museum, 1994), 13–24; Kenneth Joel Zogry, *The Best the Country Affords: Vermont Furniture, 1765–1850*, Philip Zea, ed. (Bennington, VT: The Bennington Museum, 1995).

3. Fred R. Shapiro, "Who Said, 'Go West, Young Man'—Quote Detective Debunks Myths," based on research for *Yale Book of Quotations* (New Haven: Yale University Press, 2006). According to Shapiro's research, the quote appeared in the August 25, 1838, issue of the newspaper *New Yorker*. http://www.llrx.com/features/quotedetective.htm. Accessed 1/27/2015.

4. Robinson, *Checklist*, 48, 72.

5. J. Leander Bishop, *A History of American Manufacturers from 1608 to 1860*, 3 vols. (Philadelphia: Edward Young & Company, 1868), 3:455.

6. Howard Coffin, *Full Duty: Vermonters in the Civil War* (Woodstock, VT: The Countryman Press, 1993), 356. Michigan holds the distinction of the highest per capita percentage of casualties on the Union side during the Civil War, while Vermont may have lost the highest percentage of men in battle. In 1860, the population of Vermont was 315,098. A total of 34,238 served in the various branches of the military, and 5,224 died in service.

7. Other writings on connoisseurship include: Montgomery, 48-52; E. McClung Fleming, "Artifact Study: A Proposed Model," *Winterthur Portfolio* 9 (1974): 153–73; Jules David Prown, "Style as Evidence," *Winterthur Portfolio* 15, no. 3 (Autumn 1980): 197–210; Philip D. Zimmerman, "Workmanship as Evidence: A Model for Object Study," *Winterthur Portfolio* 16, no. 4 (Winter 1981): 283–307.

8. David R. Pesuit, "Structure, Style, and Evolution: The Sack-Back Windsor Armchair," *American Furniture 2005* (Milwaukee: The Chipstone Foundation, 2005): 63–118.

9. Robinson, *Checklist*, 16.

10. Zadock Thompson, *History of Vermont, Natural, Civil, and Statistical* (Burlington, VT: Chauncey Goodrich, 1842), 209–10.

11. Thompson, 209–11.

12. Thompson, 214.

13. Thompson, 216.

14. Dean A. Fales, Jr., "Collector's Notes," *The Magazine Antiques* 98, no 4 (October 1970): 629.

15. Account book of Nathan Burnell, 1822–1866. Collection of Duane E. Merrill.

16. Nahum Parker Papers, Sheldon Museum, Middlebury, VT, Misc. File. See also Zogry, p. 57.

17. Nahum Parker Papers, Sheldon Museum, Middlebury, VT, Misc. File. See also Zogry, p. 57.

18. David Pye, *The Nature and Art of Workmanship* (Cambridge: Cambridge University Press, 1968), 1–29.

19. Zogry, 62–63.

20. John L. Scherer, *New York Furniture at the New York State Museum* (Alexandria, VA: Highland House Publishers, 1984), 70.

21. Letter, Cynthia Jones Goodrich to Norman Jones, Middlebury, VT, 5 April 1856. Jones Family Papers, Mrs. A. E. Brown, East Hubbardton, VT, Xerox copy in possession of the author. See also, N. D. Jones, "Norman Jones, Vermont Cabinetmaker," *The Magazine Antiques* 111, no. 5 (May 1977): 1028–31.

FIGURE 1
Secretary, ca. 1830
John Marshall (1787–1860), Royalton, Vermont
White pine, basswood, yellow birch, mahogany
veneer, baize, brass, and glass
H. 76 ¾ x W. 45 ¾ x D. 21 inches
Shelburne Museum, 2000–17

Rich and Tasty Furniture: Zachariah Harwood and John Marshall

Jean M. Burks

AT THE BEGINNING OF THE NINETEENTH CENTURY, elements of refinement, borrowed from America's upper classes, began to influence the lives of middle-class residents. The move toward gentility found expression in a multitude of ways: increased public school education, formal parlors furnished for personal entertaining at home, and a desire to pursue a sense of beauty in everyday life. In his seminal book *The Refinement of America: Persons, Houses, Cities* (1992), Richard L. Bushman records this advance of gentility and explores its perhaps unexpected effects on American society. By mid-century, he notes, "vernacular gentility had become the possession of the American middle class. All who aspired to simple respectability had to embody the marks of genteel style in their persons and their houses."[1] Appreciation of a genteel style came to be called *taste*. "In everyday discourse where the word had frequent usage, no effort was made to define taste, . . . and yet good taste was always admired and it was a requisite of a refined personality. Such a person recognized beauty through the exercise of the powers of discrimination and could unerringly evaluate the aesthetic qualities of a vase, an opera, a face, or a suit of clothes." The rooms and the furnishings with which these individuals chose to surround themselves defined a genteel family to society around them.[2]

A review of advertisements in early Vermont newspapers of the period reveals that the parlance of the day used to attract potential purchasers of a variety of products was the phrase "rich and tasty." In the 1829 and 1839 *Vermont Gazette*, Bennington cabinetmakers Hastings Kendrick (b. 1804) and T. Crosset respectively announced their intention to manufacture a variety of "rich and tasty furniture . . . Secretaries, Sofas, Sideboards, Bureaus, Pier, Claw, Card, and other kinds of tables."[3]

Astute independent craftsmen as well as successful entrepreneurs aspired to this "rich and tasty" sensibility in both their personal and professional endeavors. The work of Zachariah Harwood (1811–58), cabinetmaker from Rupert, Vermont, is known only through a book titled *Out of the Saltbox*, written by his great-niece, which describes the construction of a combined sawmill and gristmill at Harwood's mountaintop home at Windy Summit.[4] When the season was slack for sawing and grinding, the author's great-uncle Zach turned to making furniture. Using bird's-eye, buckhorn, violin, and curly maple, pine and cherry:

> he would make desks for himself and his brothers, and bureaus for his mother and the girls. For his father, a medicine cupboard big enough to hold a year's supply of the herbs he loved to gather, and with a drawer for every herb after it had been dried and

FIGURE 2

Slant-front Desk, ca. 1810

Attributed to John Marshall (1787–1860), Royalton, Vermont

Cherry, white pine, and replaced brass

Dimensions unknown

Former Collection Hood Museum,

Dartmouth College, F978.182

pulverized with the big iron mortar and pestle. . . . The medicine cupboard he finished first from his best white pine. A curly maple bureau with Sandwich glass knobs he fashioned next for Great-Grandmother, carefully turning the pillars and legs on his wheel-belted lathe. . . . Four drawers, each nine inches deep, the young craftsman topped by one twice the depth to hold his mother's spare coverlid and the blankets and comforter for the coldest nights of winter. He added a small drawer at each end of the broad top also, for her caps and gold beads. Great-Grandmother prized the handsome bureau, not only for its daily convenience but even more for her son's fine workmanship that went into its making. Harriet, Abigail, and Ruby, receiving theirs in turn, prized theirs as well. Harriet on her thirty-first birthday, Abigail and Ruby when, as brides, they went down the mountain to homes of their own . . .

The piece over which he worked longest was the secretary where he would keep his accounts and the numerous other items that a man with a thriving mill was always needing to keep. He fashioned its frame from the darkest strips of the wild brown cherry, its ends from the heart of a great white pine. Panels for the bookcase doors and the dropleaf for writing he smoothed from the buckhorn maple, the narrow drawer beneath and the supporting columns from his choicest piece of bird's eye. Violin maple went to the making of the two wide bottom drawers, and for the whole, hours of loving labor on these woods that he had collected as a boy from his home hill. Brown cherry knobs turned on his lathe and strap hinges cut from a pulley belt remnant completed his secretary.[5]

This detailed account leads to the following observations: "rich and tasty" furniture was made for home use as well as for sale; it was given as gifts for special occasions; it represents the maker's knowledge of current forms and styles even in a rural environment; and it exploits the characteristics of local woods selected for specific parts. Yet Zachariah Harwood's keen eye and craftsmanship have not yet identified him as a cabinetmaker in any written or visual sources other than this personal account of his activities written by a descendant.

Although John Marshall plied his trade commercially in Royalton, Vermont, his entire known output remains documented only through pieces made for, and preserved by, family and friends. His surviving, unmarked repertoire consists of a slant-front desk, a secretary, two bureaus, four thumb-back chairs, and a tall case clock, which have remained in the family continuously for five generations, providing impeccable documentation. The current owners' great-great-grandmother, Charlotte Marshall (1827–96), was the youngest daughter of John. This physical evidence, together with recorded land transactions, published histories of Royalton, and nineteenth-century census records, provides insight into Marshall's business practices, working relationships, and respected standing in the community.

An 1809 deed notes that John Marshall, then living in Hartford, Vermont, provided clockmaker Asahel Cheney of Royalton with cherry clock cases in partial payment for land.[6] In that year Marshall moved to Royalton and purchased the property and shop owned by Cheney. He continued to use the shop for his cabinetmaking business until 1825, when he acquired the Fay farm and relocated his shop to his house. According to *The History of Royalton, Vermont*: "whatever he touched seemed to turn to gold." On that topic, one of his descendants described him as "peculiar and long-headed, one who always got 'the best end of the bargain.'"[7] Accordingly, he held many mortgages, had a store in N. Royalton which he let to other merchants, and in 1822 purchased "the mills which consisted of saw, clover, grist, carding and fulling."[8] The Royalton history further reports that "he filled many town offices, served as selectman in 1834 and 1844, and was one of the solid men of the town. He was called 'Major' because he was drum major of the 2nd Regiment 4th Division of Vermont

FIGURE 3
Tall Case Clock, Royalton, Vermont, 1820–25
John Marshall (1787–1860), Royalton, Vermont
Works attributed to Asahel Cheney (1759–1819),
Royalton, Vermont
Cherry, mahogany veneers, brass
H. 97 x W. 21 x D. 10 ½ inches
Collection of the Fowler Family

militia in 1820."[9] Above all, however, "Mr. Marshall was probably the finest cabinetmaker ever in Royalton. He worked with the most expensive woods and took infinite pains in turning out handsome and elaborate articles. There still is to be found in town some of his handiwork in the shape of bureaus and other furniture which would bring large prices if found in city shops today."[10]

John Marshall was clearly aware of changing tastes. Desks of the period were complex and expensive furniture forms requiring a high degree of knowledge and craftsmanship on the part of the maker. They performed many functions, both visible and invisible. They provided work space; offered secure storage in hidden compartments for valuables such as coins, documents, and jewelry; and proclaimed the owner's taste and status. By about 1800 the slant-top desk had become old-fashioned and was infrequently made except in rural areas.[11] As English design trendsetter Thomas Sheraton noted in his 1803 *Cabinet Dictionary* under the heading of "Bureau," the term used by the English to denote a slant-top desk, these pieces of furniture "are nearly obsolete in London, at least they are so amongst fashionable people. I have, however, endeavoured to retrieve their obscurity, by adding to them an open book case, and modernizing the lower part, as in plate 23, where they are called Bureau Bookcases."[12]

This slant-front desk (Fig. 2) with a Royalton history[13] represents a passé design that was abandoned in favor of a more contemporary interpretation. Mr. Marshall's monumental secretary (Fig. 1) combining desk and bookcase functions was an unusual Vermont form, yet one that reflected current fashion. The stylish desk was now fitted with a hinged flap that folds down and rests on pull-out sliding supports (lopers). Here, the upper case is furnished with two glazed doors over three narrow drawers above a lower case with a deeply overhanging top drawer surrounded by boldly turned block and column legs in the Greco-Roman revival style. The entire facade is covered in bookmatched mahogany veneers. Based on family history and physical evidence, this piece survived the great 1927 flood while still in Royalton.[14]

Fortunately, it was located on the second floor of the current owner's grandmother's house, which came apart when the rising waters swept the lower, older section of the building down the river.[15]

There are two other Marshall case pieces still in the family's possession that define distinctive elements of his style. Following the latest trends, these four-drawer cherry bureaus were clearly inspired by current taste. One is fitted with two integral glove boxes, a scrolling backsplash, and original pressed glass pulls, similar to the one made by Zachariah Harwood and described above. When the pieces are viewed as a group, it is clear cabinetmaker Marshall had a strong interest in tall, boldly turned legs beneath bilateral engaged columns that incorporate rope and spiral turning.

As the settlement of southeastern Vermont moved up the Connecticut River, so did the demand for timepieces. Clockmakers such as Asahel Cheney (b. 1768), trained by his famous father Benjamin in a larger shop in East Hartford, Connecticut, moved north to Windham and later Windsor County, Vermont, to capture the emerging market. He is first listed in Royalton in 1806 and in 1809 cut the aforementioned deal with John Marshall to sell him property there in exchange for clock cases. From then until Cheney's death in 1819, the clockmaker's and cabinetmaker's personal lives were closely intertwined, as suggested by their collaboration on this tall case clock (Fig. 3). The pencil inscription inside the door reads "July 21 1867/John Marshall/This was my father's clock and given to me after my mother's death/April 1875/it was more than 50 years old at/that time/Charlotte Fowler." Charlotte Marshall (1827–96), who recorded this history, was the youngest daughter of John Marshall's ten children; she married Norman Fowler on May 17, 1849.

What developed in case design is a distinctive Vermont idiom based on *au courant* Connecticut models, including the scalloped skirt seen here. Although clearly Sheraton in style in the use of contrasting light cherry and dark mahogany veneers, reeded quarter columns, and geometric oval inlay centered on the door, this tall case clock shows

FIGURE 4
Detail, Tall Case Clock by John Marshall. The
Masonic imagery used on this clock case reflects
the cabinetmaker's association with clockmaker
Asahel Cheney.

John Marshall's own distinctive touches. Most striking are the four fully engaged columns with turned feet and finials that form the legs extending above the waist—an unusual treatment which is, however, reminiscent of his three other case pieces. The appearance of the two inlaid Ionic columns in dark and light contrasting woods on the base with arch above—clearly a Masonic symbol representing Solomon's Temple that rarely appears in this material—is a customized design (Fig. 4). The keystone is supported on either side by *voussoirs* (trapezoidal building blocks) and the reeded columns are broken in a way to suggest a decorative ribbon encircling them. The fact that Mr. Cheney was given a Masonic funeral after his sudden death in 1819[16] strongly suggests that the clockmaker had this case designed by his cabinetmaker colleague, John Marshall, specifically to house his own brass movement. As it may have been for personal use and not for sale, Cheney did not need to record his name on the dial. Presumably at some point after his burial in the North Royalton cemetery, his bespoke timepiece was returned to the cabinetmaker and has remained with Marshall descendants to this day.

These recently discovered written references to Zachariah Harwood and physical works by John Marshall reveal the fashionable designs and urbane forms produced in the Green Mountain State and provide an introduction to the surprising range of "Rich and Tasty Furniture" made both for home use and for sale which is further explored in this catalogue.

1. Richard L. Bushman, *The Refinement of America: Persons, Houses, Cities* (New York: Alfred A Knopf, 1992), xiii.

2. Bushman, *The Refinement of America*, 83.

3. Charles A. Robinson, *Vermont Cabinetmakers & Chairmakers Before 1855: A Checklist* (Shelburne, VT: Shelburne Museum, 1994). See also Fultonhistory.com/New York NY American for the Country 1842–43: "The New London Packet Ship Victoria . . . Her 'tween decks are more lofty than any we remember to have seen—her ladies' cabin, with its stained glass windows and rich and tasty furniture, a perfect *boudoir*—so that we must e'en think a lady's eye has suggested and supervised it." See also the *Vermont Phoenix* (Brattleboro) 11/1, 15, 22/ and 12/13/1839 and *Bellows Falls Gazette* 11/2, 9, 23/1839 advertisement for "Wheeler & Miller, New firm, New Store and New Goods—New Styles, English, French and American prints, very rich and tasty patterns."

4. Ruth Hersey, *Out of the Saltbox* (Chicago and New York: Rand McNally and Company, 1962).

5. Hersey, 181–83.

6. November 23, 1809, land transaction between John Marshall and Asahel Cheney, Windsor County Registry of Deeds, Windsor County Courthouse. Secondary source, Robinson, *Checklist*, 76.

7. Evelyn M. Wood Lovejoy, *The History of Royalton Vermont, with family genealogies 1769–1911* (Burlington, VT: Free Press Print. Co., 1911), 871.

8 . Lovejoy, 401.

9. Lovejoy, 871.

10. Lovejoy, 421.

11. Charles F. Montgomery, *American Furniture: The Federal Period* (New York: The Viking Press, 1966), 217.

12. Thomas Sheraton, *Cabinet Directory*, Charles F. Montgomery, ed. (New York: Praeger Publishers, 1970), 111.

13. Margaret J. Moody, *American Decorative Arts at Dartmouth* (Hanover, NH: The Trustees of Dartmouth College, 1981), 16.

14. "Known as one of Vermont's most devastating events, after three days of heavy rain in November of that year, the resulting deluge took out 1285 bridges, miles of roads and railroads, and countless homes and buildings. Eighty-four people perished in the disaster, including Lt. Governor S. Hollister Jackson." http://www.uvm.edu/landscape/1927_flood/about_1927_flood.htm

15. It suffered surface damage to the legs and some veneer and glazing losses, which have been subsequently repaired by Shelburne Museum's conservator after the piece was donated by the Marshall descendants.

16. Lovejoy, 717. Cheney became a first degree Mason 7/20/1796 and second degree 8/17/1796 at the Harmony Lodge in the Northfield, Massachusetts [MA] area. There is no information regarding his attaining third degree status, according to the records at the Grand Lodge of Massachusetts in Boston.

A Catalogue of Vermont Furniture

Setting the Scene

———

After the completion of the Champlain and Erie canals in 1823 and 1825, Burlington entered a period of brisk growth that transformed the town into Vermont's largest city. Burlington became a lumbering and manufacturing center and one of the most powerful mill sites in the region. Wharves located on Lake Champlain provided easy access to international water-borne trade and allowed steamboats to connect freight and passengers with the Rutland and Burlington and Vermont Central Railroads.

This pastel was probably copied from a print that appeared in *Graham's Magazine,* 1852,[1] or from a print after an original drawing by Thomas Addison Richards that appeared in the volume *American Scenery* in 1854.[2] The depiction of the Unitarian Church at the head of Church Street in white rather than red brick suggests that this artist never set foot in Burlington.[3]

———

1. *Graham's American Monthly Magazine of Literature and Art* (July 1848–June 1856), vol. III, 1852.
2. Thomas Addison Richards, *American Scenery* (New York: George A. Leavitt), 223.
3. Per a 12/17/14 conversation with Bob Furrer, facilities manager of the Unitarian Church, the exterior was always brick.

FIGURE 1

View of Burlington, 1852–60
Pastel on paper
19 x 28 inches
Shelburne Museum 1964–174 and 27.3.2–8
*This townscape shows Burlington Bay, with Rock Point
at the right, bustling with both leisure time (sailboats)
and commercial (steamship) activity.*

CATALOGUE 1
Cradle, Brandon, Vermont, ca. 1800
Richardson Family
Wrought iron
H. 30 x W. 16 ¾ x D. 36 inches
Shelburne Museum, 1991–9

CATALOGUE 1

Not all Vermont furniture is crafted of wood. This unique cradle associated with the Richardson family of blacksmiths in Brandon was wrought of iron, rather than created from wooden parts. Nevertheless, it was assembled with standard mortise-and-tenon construction, and with uprights terminating in mushroom-shaped caps in the manner of a joiner.

It was not extraordinary for trained woodworkers to turn their talents toward metalwork. Osman Combs, a native of Townshend, was employed as a chairmaker from 1843 to 1850, when he took over a blacksmith shop and transferred his skills to that trade. Conversely, Erastus Cook, who was employed as a blacksmith for thirty years in Brookfield, was listed as a chairmaker in an 1856 Business Directory.[1]

1. Charles A. Robinson, *Vermont Cabinetmakers & Chairmakers Before 1855: A Checklist* (Shelburne, VT: Shelburne Museum, 1994), 43.

Cradle, Barnet, Vermont, ca. 1820
Darius Harvey (b. 1802)
Branded: "Harvey, D. Passumsic"
Ash, white pine, maple, basswood and paint
H. 30 ¾ x W. 14 ¾ x D. 34 inches
Shelburne Museum, 1984–68

CATALOGUE 2

Built for rocking from front to back rather than from side to side like most juvenile sleeping furniture, this innovative cradle takes its cue from Windsor design. The plank bottom, step-down crest rail, and rungs incised and painted in imitation of bamboo were created from templates for a child's rod-back Windsor chair. The maker, Darius Harvey of Barnet, probably learned the trade in the cabinetmaking shop of his father, Ira Harvey (1772–1834), and expanded his line of Windsor furniture until he took over the Passumsic Hotel in Barnet in 1832.[1]

1. C. Santore, *The Windsor Style in America* (Philadelphia: Running Press, 1987) vol. 2, 253, and Robinson, *Checklist*, 61.

Recalling the Eighteenth Century

CATALOGUE 3

The inscription on this chest follows the convention of important early eighteenth-century case furniture from Hadley, Massachusetts, constructed specifically to celebrate a marriage[1] and sets the stage for a number of newly discovered nineteenth-century Vermont pieces documenting the specific origin of the materials used (see Cat. 31). This chest's inscription represents a link between past and future cabinet-making traditions. Despite the detailed written information, it is not possible to identify the maker. Charles Robinson, born in Coventry, Connecticut, in 1761, was married in 1785 to Chloe Dart (b. 1765) of Bolton, Connecticut, by her father, then an assistant judge of Windsor County in Weathersfield, Vermont.[2] There are no eighteenth-century documented carpenters or cabinetmakers of that name in this town, and this chest may be the only record of its maker.[3]

The seven graduated and beaded drawers are anchored at the top by a complex molding and at the bottom by a dovetailed bracket base with spurs and unusually large feet. It boasts the original finish and turned knobs that were probably added later for ease of access. The careful selection of figured cherry on the drawers predicts the prefer-ence in the Green Mountain State for dramatic native woods—a trend which would be repeated throughout the nineteenth century.

1. Philip Zea and Suzanne L. Flynt, *Hadley Chests* (Deerfield, MA: Memorial Hall Museum, 1992); Philip Zea, "The Fruits of Oligarchy: Patronage and the Hadley Chest Tradition in Western Mas-sachusetts," *New England Furniture: Essays in Memory of Benno M. Forman*, ed. Brock Jobe (Boston: Society for the Preservation of New England Antiquities, 1987).
2. www.findagrave.com /Charles Robinson (1761–1827).
3. Charles A. Robinson, *Vermont Cabinetmakers & Chairmakers Before 1855: A Checklist* (Shelburne, VT: Shelburne Museum, 1994), 125.

CATALOGUE 3
Chest of Drawers, Weathersfield, Vermont, 1785
Attributed to Dart
Inscription: Written in pencil on bottom of top proper left drawer bottom by
George R. Larned: "This case of drawers was made for Chloe (Dart) Robinson
by her father [name unknown] Dart in Wethersfield Vt about the time of her
marriage in 1785 [to Charles Robinson] out of cherry boards from trees on
his farm. She was mother of Clarissa [Robinson] Larned and grandmother of
George R. Larned."
Cherry and eastern white pine
H. 56 ¾ x W. 40 ¾ x D. 18 ¼ inches
Private Collection

CATALOGUE 4
Side Chair, Bennington, Vermont, 1790s
H. 39 x W. 19 x D. 15 ½ inches
Yellow birch, paint, and rush
Private Collection

44

CATALOGUE 4

This side chair, one of a pair found in Norwich, Vermont, is associated in both design and construction with an unnamed Bennington shop in operation during the last quarter of the eighteenth century.[1] The chair is distantly related to Eastern Massachusetts models in the splat design and crestrail with upturned ends.[2] However, this Bennington version is distinguished by the consistent placement of the front stretcher between the front legs and above the top of the side stretchers and by the shortened backsplat. It is finished with Spanish brown paint over hardwoods and has a rush seat. Progressively more expensive examples have survived, made of solid cherry with beaded rails and upholstered slip seats to suit the purchaser's pocketbook.

1. Kenneth Joel Zogry, *The Best the Country Affords: Vermont Furniture 1765–1850*, Philip Zea, ed. (Bennington, VT: The Bennington Museum, 1995), 31.
2. *The Great River, Art & Society of the Connecticut Valley, 1635–1820*, Gerald W. R. Ward and William N. Hosley, Jr., eds. (Hartford, CT: Wadsworth Atheneum, 1985), cat. 120.

CATALOGUE 5

Chest, Brookfield, Vermont, 1810
Eastern white pine
H. 20 ¼ x W. 39 ½ x D. 13 ¼ inches
Private Collection

CATALOGUE 5

This relatively small six-board chest with intact till is functional as well as attractive. The eye-catching decorative elements are the shaped ends and the geometric chip carving on both ends of the lid and the front board. Chip carving is executed using knives or chisels to make angled cuts into wood to remove small pieces of the material to form a pattern. This technique has a long and rich history practiced in most countries over many centuries. In America, chip carving is most often used with soft, secondary woods like basswood, or pine. The fact that this box was found in Brookfield, Vermont, provides the only clue to its possible origin.

46

CATALOGUE 6

At first glance, the conservative design of this high chest relates to Massachusetts antecedents of the mid-eighteenth century in the drawer arrangement, the shaped skirt with drop pendants, and the attenuated cabriole legs terminating in pad feet. Although the chest is unsigned, distinctive construction features suggest that it bears the imprint of the Dunlap family of cabinetmakers, who worked in the Bedford and Salisbury, New Hampshire, area. More specifically, the drawer bottoms are rabbeted, rather than beveled to the sides of the drawers, and wooden pins are employed throughout instead of nails, which encourage splitting.[1]

The high chest descended from Daniel Benedict Dutton (1773–1849), who relocated from Woodstock, Vermont, to Dutton Hill in Norwich, Vermont, where the chest remained for nearly two centuries. It was apparently made for Dutton by one of many furniture makers who migrated from eastern New England and were familiar with the workshops of the Dunlap family of southern New Hampshire.[2]

1. Robinson, *Checklist*, 15.
2. Archibald Dunlap (1781–1825), the second son of Major John Dunlap (1746–92), appears in period records as a joiner and in fact moved to Hartland, Vermont, in 1818; see Robinson, *Checklist*, 49.

48

CATALOGUE 7

Vermont's early tradesmen were jacks of all trades and practiced a diversity of occupations that included, among other things, framing buildings, farming, and furniture making.[1]

Without the inscription, this conservative six-drawer chest with bracket base firmly rooted in the Chippendale style would be considered generic, mid-eighteenth-century, rural New England furniture. It reflects the training of a housewright in the use of thick stock appropriate for architectural paneling, straightforward joinery, and an architectural cornice.[2] The brass knobs, rather than turned wooden pulls, however, are surprising. John Cardwill, the self-proclaimed maker, was listed as a resident of Middletown in the 1810 Federal census, although nothing further is known of his activities. This is the only surviving documentation of his work and the earliest piece of Vermont furniture that bears a full inscription.

1. William N. Hosley, Jr., "Vermont Furniture 1790–1830," *New England Furniture: Essays in Memory of Benno N. Forman*, ed. Brock Jobe (Boston: Society for the Preservation of New England Antiquities, 1987), 247.
2. Hosley, 247.

A Legacy of Specialization: Chairmaking

CATALOGUE 8

Although painted fancy chairs with flag and cane seats were advertised by Burlington makers John Abbott and Thomas Wood, Samuel Nichols and John Herrick, and Charles Nelson,[1] scenic decoration rarely appears. This chair, originally part of a set of twelve, is one of three that have survived with remarkable historic and artistic documentation. An article in *The Free Press* dated March 22, 1866, reports on the sale of the contents of the Bank of Burlington, including "twelve Director's chairs, each having on its broad back rail a small painting of some noticeable building or residence in Burlington. . . . They were the work of a Mr. Curtis, who in those days found exercise for his genius chiefly in the decoration of clock cases, manufactured in Burlington by Curtis and Dunning." Each of the scenes is described, including the one shown here depicting the 1801 Main Building of the University of Vermont, which burned in 1824, as well as the 1808 Jewett House, which became a hotel, and the 1822 Bank of Burlington, which was closed in 1866.[2]

Clearly commissioned by savvy patrons to celebrate the town's architectural achievements, this chair attests to Burlington's rise as an artistic center.

1. Charles A. Robinson *Vermont Cabinetmakers & Chairmakers Before 1855: A Checklist* (Shelburne, VT: Shelburne Museum, 1994), 26, 80, 81.
2. Kenneth Joel Zogry, *The Best the Country Affords* (Bennington, VT: The Bennington Museum, 1995), 73, footnote 3.

CATALOGUE 8

Fancy Chair, Burlington, Vermont, ca. 1822
Attributed to Samuel Nichols (1793–1869) and John Herrick
(1792–1839) or John Abbott (1792–1839) and Thomas Wood
(ca. 1798–date unknown)
Decoration attributed to Charles Curtis (1801–76)
Painted white pine, ash, and basswood
H. 32 ¾ x W. 17 x D. 15 ¾ inches
Fleming Museum of Art, University of Vermont
Gift of Mr. and Mrs. Levi Smith, Jr., 1980.6.1

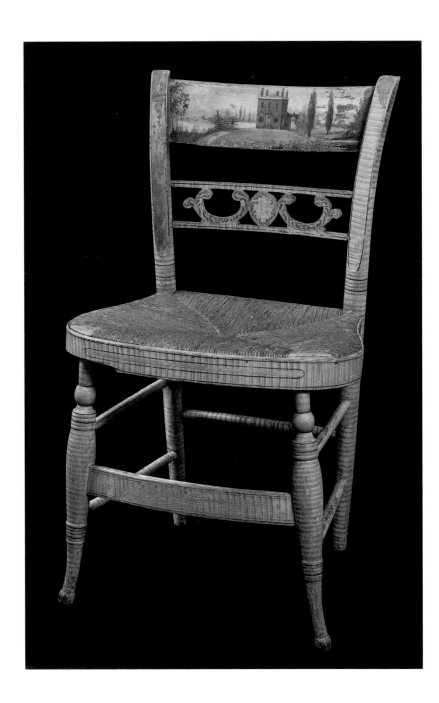

CATALOGUE 9
Chair, Springfield, Vermont, ca. 1820
Ephraim Burpee (b. 1784)
Painted hardwoods
H. 31 x W. 18 ½ x D. 17 inches
Shelburne Museum, 1993–21

CATALOGUE 9

This Windsor chair has the paper label "Windsor Chairs, Made & Sold/ by/Ephraim Burpee/Weathersfield, Vermont" with the word "Springfield" hand-written over the printed word "Weathersfield." Ephraim may have been born in Sterling, Massachusetts, where he learned his trade as part of the large Burpee family of chairmakers there. Furniture makers in Sterling specialized in wooden-seated chairs characterized by bamboo-turned legs and a thick plank seat, although marked examples are rare.[1] Ephraim Burpee is listed in the 1820 Weathersfield census before apparently moving to nearby Springfield, where he lived and worked.[2]

According to another typed paper label affixed underneath the seat, at one point this chair was owned by Emily Jane Dutton Proctor (1835–1915) and came from the 1782 Dutton House in Cavendish, Vermont, which was moved to the Shelburne Museum campus in 1950. When the chair was acquired, it was covered in black paint that was subsequently removed to reveal the original straw yellow surface and freehand dark red and green decoration on the crest and seat front. Pale yellow was the ideal choice for the simulated bamboo chair. Flowers and fruits were the most popular decorative motifs for the Windsor crest during the early decades of the nineteenth century.[3] The conservator observes that the chair once had a comb, now missing, and longer legs which have since been cut down.

1. Donna Keith Baron, "Furniture Makers and Retailers in Worcester County, Massachusetts, Working to 1850," in *The Magazine Antiques*, May, 1993, 784–95. Also see Frank G. White, "Sterling, Massachusetts: An Early Nineteenth-Century Seat of Chairmaking," in *Rural New England Furniture: People, Place, and Production*, The Dublin Seminar for New England Folklife Annual Proceedings, 1998, ed. Peter Benes (Boston: Boston University, 1998), 119–37.
2. Charles Horace Hubbard and Justus Dartt, *History of the Town of Springfield, Vermont: with a genealogical record*, 1895 (Boston: G. H. Walker & Co.), 52. "The first house was built by Abigail Lyndes, not far from 1820 . . . the next . . .1831. . . . The next was occupied by Mr. Eaton, afterward used as a chair shop by Ephraim Burpee."
3. Nancy Goyne Evans, *American Windsor Furniture, Specialized Forms* (New York: Hudson Hills Press in association with the Henry Francis du Pont Winterthur Museum, 1997), pl. 17.

CATALOGUE 10 AND 11

Identifying Vermont-made Windsor chairs and sorting them into groups is difficult. However, these two rockers were acquired from the Paul family, first mentioned in Woodstock and Pomfret in the late eighteenth century as prominent leaders and businessmen.[1] The chairs' continuous descent to the current owner suggests they did not stray far from their place of origin.

The primary chairmaker active in Woodstock from 1838 to 1865 was native-born John White (1803–65) whose father, Francis (1757–1839), had settled in the area by 1800. In 1839 John advertised in the *Vermont Mercury* "a great variety of Chairs, for sale on reasonable terms."[2] Although no seating marked by this maker has come to light, the Woodstock Historical Society has published several side chairs, rockers, and a bench attributed to him based on oral and local owner-ship history.[3] Shared characteristics include step-down crests, raked back spindles, and scroll arms slightly splayed outward, supported on spindles.

The 1850 census records John White as a painter, a term which may refer to his trade as a decorative artist and stenciler—skills which he may have plied on this comb-back fancy rocking chair (see Cat. 10).

---

1. Henry Hobart Vail, *Pomfret Vermont*, vol. II (Boston: Cockayne, 1930), 350.
2. Robinson, *Checklist*, 110.
3. Janet Houghton and Corwin Sharp, *Made in Woodstock, Furniture in the Collection of the Woodstock Historical Society* (Woodstock, VT: The Woodstock Historical Society, 1997), 30–40.

CATALOGUE 10
Comb-back Windsor Chair, Woodstock, Vermont, ca. 1825
Mixed woods and paint
H. 41 x W. 17 ¾ x D. 19 ½ inches
Private Collection

CATALOGUE 11
Windsor Rocking Chair, Woodstock, Vermont, ca. 1825
Mixed woods and paint
H. 32 ½ x W. 21 ½ x D. 16 ½ inches
Private Collection

56

CATALOGUE 12

Franklin County in northwestern Vermont borders Canada and is about fifty miles south of Montreal. During the Embargo of 1807–09, which banned trade with Great Britain, and for many years afterward, Montreal played an important role in the economy of western Vermont. There are several instances of Vermont cabinetmakers migrating north.[1] Conversely, distinct elements of the Louis XV style popular in French Canada made their way into Vermont, as seen in the curving crest rail of this "salamander"-inspired side chair.[2] It is further embellished with ball turnings on the back spindles and bamboo indentations on the front legs. This is one of a pair that descended in the Sanborn family of Franklin County, Vermont.[3]

1. See Hosley, 254, and Ross Fox, "Julius Barnard (1769–after 1820) as Peripatetic Yankee Cabinetmaker," in *Vermont History*, vol. 79, No.1 (Winter/Spring 2011), 1–25.
2. Michael S. Bird, *Canadian Country Furniture 1675–1950* (Toronto: Stoddard Publishing Co., Limited, 1994), #221 and 222 chairs *à la capucine*.
3. Jeremiah Sanburn of Swanton is listed in the 1820 and 1830 censuses and Daniel Sanbourn/Sanburn of St. Albans appears in the 1820 and 1830 censuses.

Comb-back Rocking Chair, ca. 1825
Attributed to John Saxton, Shelburne Falls, Vermont
Basswood (seat) and mixed hardwoods
H. 40 x W. 22 x D. 32 inches (including rockers)
Collection of J. Brooks Buxton

CATALOGUE 13

Based on oral history, a chairmaker named Saxton produced Windsor comb-back seating during the first quarter of the nineteenth century. Records show the presence of Nehemiah (1771–1871), Horace (1779–1848), and James Saxton (1776–1848) as residents of Shelburne in the 1810 and 1820 United States censuses but offer little information about their occupations.[1] Distinct design and construction features on attributed examples include a notched crest rail; arms terminating in a three-finger "knuckle" with the lower half made from a carved and applied block of wood, pinned from above; and a medial stretcher containing a three-dimensional oval medallion.[2] The broad seats of most Saxton chairs are constructed in two pieces. Applied to the face of the principal plank is a narrow section of wood held in place by two large, square wooden pins visible at the front edge near each leg. This particular chair is distinguished by its elegant elongated rockers.

1. Robinson, *Checklist*, 95.
2. See Nancy Goyne Evans, *American Windsor Furniture Specialized Forms* (New York: Hudson Hills Press, 1997), 62.

57

Side Chair, 1842
Ara Howe (1797–1863), Brookfield, Vermont
Painted and stenciled maple, eastern white pine, and sycamore
H. 33 x W. 15 ½ x D. 14 ½ inches
Shelburne Museum, 1991–37.1–2

CATALOGUE 14

This is one of a pair of fancy chairs with paper label affixed beneath the sharply chamfered seat that clearly proclaims its origins: "MANUFAC-TURED BY/ARA HOWE/BROOKFIELD,VT./WARRANTED." Howe emigrated from Sterling, Massachusetts, one of the largest chairmaking communities in New England, to Brookfield, Vermont, in 1841 and in 1849 was listed by the New England Mercantile Union Business Directory as a chairmaker and furniture maker in that town.[1] According to the handwritten inscription, the chairs were "Bought by C. S. Doyle when he went to housekeeping in 1842." Vital records research suggests that Christopher S. Dole (b. 1815) of Northfield, who married Harriet Howe, was the original recipient of these chairs.[2]

The chairs feature Gothic-style cut-outs in the crest rail and gold floral and vine stencil decoration over a black ground that imitates japanning. Apparently Oriental style was popular in eighteenth-century Vermont. As early as 1808 Luther Holbrook (1780–) of Brattleboro advertised "fashionable gilt, jappanned [*sic*] or painted fancy, bamboo, fanback, and common chairs,"[3] and in 1812 Thomas Boynton of Hartland offered "a general assortment of Japanned furniture—consisting of a few hundred warranted strong, fancy top, Double and single top, Bamboo, Windsor and dining chairs of various colours."[4] The lyre shape on the splat is a popular motif and another direct furniture reference to classical antiquity (see Cat. 39).

---

1. *New England Mercantile Union Business Directory*, New York: Pratt & Co., 1849.
2. Shelburne Museum object files, notes by Curator Lauren B. Hewes, September 23, 1991.
3. Robinson, *Checklist*, 64.
4. Robinson, *Checklist*, 35–36.

Neoclassical Vermont

CATALOGUE 15

Following his training as a clockmaker with his father Benjamin Cheney in East Hartford, Connecticut, Martin Cheney, a brother of Asahel, relocated in 1803 to Windsor, Vermont, where he remained until 1809 to take advantage of a developing market. This sophisticated and expensive timepiece combines features associated with urban clockmaking traditions found in Connecticut as well as in Massachusetts. The integration of an engraved brass dial from Cheney's previous clockmaking experience with the kidney dial shelf clock form, introduced by the Willard family in Boston during the 1790s, represents an unusual high-style presence in Vermont.[1] The two-part case supported on French feet was probably purchased from an unidentified local cabinetmaker.

1. *The Great River. Art & Society of the Connecticut Valley 1635–1820*, eds. Gerald W. R. Ward and William N. Hosley, Jr. (Hartford, CT: Wadsworth Atheneum, 1985), cat. 242.

CATALOGUE 15
Shelf Clock, Windsor, Vermont, ca. 1805
Martin Cheney (1778–ca. 1830)
Movement: eight-day, brass and steel; case: mahogany,
white pine, mahogany veneer, light and dark wood inlay
H. 18 x W. 9 ½ x D. 3 ⅞ inches
From the collections of The Henry Ford

CATALOGUE 16

The elliptical form of the dressing table with mahogany as the primary wood was offered in early nineteenth-century Portsmouth, New Hampshire.[1] This example with mahogany veneer and straight, rather than turned and reeded, legs is inspired by the urban form purchased by wealthy seacoast merchants and entrepreneurs. Perhaps the unidentified Vermont maker had access to pattern books from English designers, such as plate 14 from *Gillow Furniture Designs 1760–1800*,[2] and abstracted and simplified the three-dimensional reality (see Fig. 16B). If he was not used to translating printed pictures to actual objects, the legs in this very stylish drawing could be read and executed as knife-blade thin, as they physically appear on this table. The hourglass inlay on the top of the legs relates to documented case pieces from Windsor, suggesting the Vermont county of origin.[3] The appearance of ink stains inside the subdivided drawer implies this piece was used as a desk at some point later in its history.

According to the information written on the underside of the drawer: "This Dressing Table was once the property of my Grandmother's sister – Mrs. Abigail [Roberts] Morton / [Morton is crossed out and True written above it] / True Cleveland (twice married) familiarly known as "Aunt Nabby" / Born December 12–1792 / Died Knowlton P.Q. 1880 / Arthur E. Richardson / 1913."

Genealogical research shows that Thomas Cleveland (1769–1861) and his wife Anna Craft (1772–1835) in 1794 arrived in Hartland "immediately after his marriage, where he cleared a fine farm, which by subsequent purchases he increased to the size of several hundred acres. They always lived in Hartland, where all their [eleven] children were born."[4] Was this table made nearby sometime after their marriage and settlement in Hartland? Following Anna's death in 1835, Thomas married Abigail Roberts True (1792–1880) of Plainfield, New Hampshire, and Bolton, Province of Quebec, where she died in 1880. Perhaps she married a "True" after Thomas's death. This prized possession passed from Anna to Abigail and then to Abigail's sister and by descent to Arthur E. Richardson, Abigail's grand-nephew. Presumably Abigail's sister's family remained in the Plainfield-Hartland area, where the table was acquired by the current owner.

1. Brock Jobe, *Portsmouth Furniture: Masterworks from the New Hampshire Seacoast* (Boston: Society for the Preservation of New England Antiquities, 1992), 147.
2. Lindsay Boynton (Royston, Herts: Bloomfield Press, 1995), PL 14.
3. Kenneth Joel Zogry, *The Best the Country Affords: Vermont Furniture 1765–1850* (Bennington, Vermont: The Bennington Museum, 1995), fig. 62.
4. James Crafts and William Crafts: *A Genealogical and Biographical History of the Descendants of Griffin and Alice Craft, of Roxbury, Mass., 1630–1890* (Northampton, MA: Gazetteer Printing Company, 1893), 226–27.

CATALOGUE 16
Lady's Dressing Table, probably Windsor, Vermont, ca. 1810
Inscribed: Painted under top of table "Mrs. A Cleveland, Hartland VT"
Mahogany, mahogany veneer, basswood, and eastern white pine
H. 31 x W. 36 x D. 17 inches; drawer 3 ¼ inches deep
Private Collection

CATALOGUE 17
Sideboard, Windsor, Vermont, 1805–09
Attributed to Julius Barnard (1769–after 1820)
Hanover, New Hampshire, or Windsor, Vermont
Cherry, cherry and mahogany veneers, whitewood inlays,
eastern white pine, and brass
H. 39 ¾ x W. 74 ½ x D. 28 ½ inches
Private Collection

The mahogany version of this sideboard currently at the Hood Museum of Art at Dartmouth College originally belonged to Mills Olcott, the treasurer of the college from 1816 to 1822. He was a prominent Hanover lawyer and businessman and in 1801 exchanged goods and services with Julius Barnard, who briefly operated a cabinetmaking shop in town.[1] In 1802 Barnard relocated his trade to Windsor, Vermont, where, in 1805, he advertised the sale of "sash-cornered, commode & strait-front Sideboards, Secretaries and Bookcases; Ladies' Writing Desks and Bookcases; circular and strait front Bureaus; card and Pembroke Tables; dining and breakfast Tables; circular and octagon end Tables; Candlestands; Clockcases; . . . Bedsteads; Sofas; lolling & easy Chairs . . . "[2] In 1809 he moved to Montreal, Canada, and in 1812 sold his stock, which according to the *Montreal Herald* included "an elegant mahogany Sideboard . . . Sopha with arms . . . a curled Maple Secretary, 35 new eight day Clocks, with and without cases . . . Mahogany 4 post Beadsteads with curtains . . . compleat assortment of Cabinet, Joiners and Carpenters tools, Several hundred pieces of boards, among which are mahogany, curled Maple & Cherry."[3] Barnard's sudden sale and exodus from Canada followed the United States' declaration of war against Great Britain, which forced Barnard to flee Montreal, a British Colony, and relocate to Pittsfield, Massachusetts, where he would remain for at least the next eight years. Following a succession of legal difficulties and financial adversity he left the Commonwealth for parts unknown, living the remainder of his life in obscurity.[4]

The elegant lines and sophisticated craftsmanship of this Hepplewhite sideboard with serpentine front on square tapering legs demonstrate that its maker was attuned to the high-style furniture fashions emanating from larger urban centers. In the 1780s Barnard originally apprenticed with Eliphalet Chapin (1741–1807), who operated a large furniture shop in East Windsor, Connecticut, where he learned the Philadelphia style, and then traveled to New York City, an experience which introduced him to "the latest and most elegant patterns for Chairs and Cabinet Work."[5]

The innovative arrangement of inlays on this piece, including the upside-down bellflowers and pendant icicles down the front legs, and the light and dark corner inlay fans (see Cat. 17B), represent Barnard's unique contribution to the rural cabinetmaking tradition in the Green Mountain State.

CATALOGUE 17B
Detail, Sideboard attributed to Julius Barnard, showing inverted bellflowers and pendant icicles on leg and fan inlay on drawers.

1. Dartmouth College, Hanover, New Hampshire, Hood Museum of Art object acquisition information, F.980.64

2. Charles A. Robinson, *Vermont Cabinetmakers & Chairmakers Before 1855: A Checklist* (Shelburne, VT: Shelburne Museum, 1994), 31.

3. Dartmouth College, Hanover, New Hampshire, Hood Museum object acquisition information, F.980.64.

4. Ross Fox, "Julius Barnard (1769–after 1820) as Peripatetic Yankee Cabinetmaker," *Vermont History*, vol. 79, No.1 (Winter/Spring 2011), 18–19.

5. Advertisement in the *Hampshire Gazette* (Northampton, MA), December 5, 1792 in Fox, 3.

CATALOGUE 18

Half Sideboard, Windsor, Vermont, 1813

Rufus Norton (1783–1818)

Inscription: Written in red pencil on side of proper left bottle drawer:
"1813/L [C?)H &/Rufus Norton/Windsor" [via black light]

Cherry, cherry and maple veneers, butternut (?) inlay, eastern white
pine, and brass

H. 43 ⅜ x W. 43 ¾ x D. 18 ¾ inches

Private Collection

CATALOGUE 18B

Detail, Rufus Norton Half Sideboard, showing inscription
written in red pencil on side of proper left bottle drawer:
"1813/L [C?)H &/Rufus Norton/Windsor" [via black light].

CATALOGUE 19
Bureau, Windsor, Vermont, 1810–15
Attributed to Rufus Norton (1783–1818)
Cherry, yellow birch, cherry veneer, mahogany and birch inlays,
basswood, brass
H. 35 ⅝ x W. 41 ½ x D. 19 ⅜ inches
Private Collection

CATALOGUE 18 AND 19

Closely related in form and decoration, these two case pieces were created in Windsor, Vermont, by Rufus Norton and are the only known works by this cabinetmaker. He formed a partnership with Julius Barnard from 1806 to 1809 (see Cat. 17) and in 1807 they advertised "Barnard & Norton are making . . . at their shop . . . every kind of Mahogany and Cherry Furniture, and Chairs of all kinds."[1] Barnard moved to Montreal in 1809 and the business was carried on by Norton, perhaps in partnership with the unidentified L [or C] H. Both the half sideboard and bureau share identical flaring French feet, a shaped skirt, and the distinctive swag and tassel inlaid frieze which is an application of neoclassical ornament found on some painted and stenciled interior wall borders of New England houses.[2] The long drawers on both pieces are fitted with corner semicircular inlays of contrasting wood which have fully evolved into fan motifs on this bureau (see Cat. 19).

The top boards of the sideboard and bureau are nailed to the case below and plugged respectively with circular or diamond-shaped pieces in contrasting wood, suggesting the craftsmanship of the same workshop.

1. Robinson, *Checklist*, 31 and 83.
2. See Stencil House, Columbus, New York, 1810–1830, Shelburne Museum.

CATALOGUE 20
Bureau, ca. 1815
Attributed to George Stedman (1795–1881), Norwich, Vermont
Cherry, maple, eastern white pine, and brass
H. 35 x W. 41 ½ x D. 19 ¾ inches
Historic Deerfield, Inc. 2011.19
Museum Collections Fund

CATALOGUE 20

The attribution of this bureau is based on the bureau signed "Made by G. Stedman/Norwich VT" in the collection of the Winterthur Museum. The Winterthur example is made of cherry and white pine with mahogany veneer and light and dark wood inlay consisting of four inset fans with wavy segments on the top surface and on all four corners of each of the drawers.[1] This example is fitted with stringing along the top edge and the drawer bottoms. An accompanying note describing where the piece was found reads in part: "in with 'attic discards' at Westlands, in South Royalton, Vermont, the Farm owned by Frank S. and Ellen W. Ainsworth. Rescued by their daughter, Ida Ainsworth Cole in 1916 . . . ."[2] It was probably made at the conclusion of the War of 1812 for a member of the Ainsworth-West families of Norwich and Royalton, Vermont.[3] The origin of the expensive bombé form with flaring French feet joined by a shaped skirt was inspired by Louis XV designs imported from Paris to Boston. Despite the fact that several Vermont makers in Guilford, Windsor, Middlebury, and Woodstock advertise "swelled cases with drawers,"[4] only six known examples survive in public (at Winterthur, Historic Deerfield, the Bennington Museum, the Henry Ford Museum, and in private collections).[5] As furniture historian William Hosley observed in 1987, the "bow-front chest of drawers is one of the most innovative examples of Vermont federal furniture."[6]

1. Charles F. Montgomery, *American Furniture: The Federal Period in the Henry Francis du Pont Winterthur Museum* (New York: Viking Press, 1966), 189–190, #147.
2. Robert W. Skinner Inc., 14 August, 2011, Sale 2558M, *American Furniture and Fine Arts* (Marlborough, Massachusetts), lot 5.
3. Deerfield accession information 2011.19.
4. Robinson, *Checklist*, see Luther Ames, Cowdery & Dutton, Calvin Elmer and Israel Huntington.
5. According to Zogry, 119.
6. William N. Hosley, Jr., "Vermont Furniture, 1790–1830," *New England Furniture: Essays in Memory of Benno Forman*, ed. Brock Jobe (Boston: Society for the Preservation of New England Antiquities, 1987), 264.

CATALOGUE 21

The remnants of this table's printed paper label read "S. Stow Cabinet-maker Near the mark [et]," although it is unclear in which town Samuel Stow conducted his trade at this time. In 1799 he advertised that he "has removed his business three doors north of Park Street on the Main Street [Windsor] where he continues the Cabinet Making Business in all its branches," but by 1805 he had moved to nearby Woodstock.[1]

This very elegant card table with fifth swing leg attributed to western Vermont and New York craftsmanship is distinguished by the variety of contrasting inlay which includes stringing and rope outline on the top edge, an astragal panel centering a contrasting oval on the apron, stiles headed with sophisticated urns (probably purchased elsewhere) enclosed in oval panels, and square tapering legs edged with stringing terminating in stylized leaves above and sawtooth cuffs below. The most remarkable observation is that the entire card table—top surface and all edges and legs—is veneered, perhaps in an effort on the part of the maker to deceive the buyer into thinking he was purchasing solid mahogany. Or perhaps the knowledgeable customer consciously purchased a less expensive model that impersonated a more costly counterpart in order to impress his social milieu.

1. Robinson, *Checklist*, 100.

Card Table, Windsor or Woodstock, Vermont, ca. 1805
Samuel Stow (born between 1756 and 1774)
H. 28 x W. 36 x D. 18 inches
Mahogany veneer and inlays, eastern white pine
Private Collection

Card Tables, 1811–14, Walpole, New Hampshire
Jonathan Eastman, Walpole, New Hampshire, and Brattleboro, Vermont
Inscription: Signed in pencil inside the apron:
"Jonathan Eastman Walpole New Hampshire"
Mahogany, mahogany and birch veneers, maple, eastern white pine
H. 29 ¼ x W. 34 ¾ x D. 17 ¾ inches
Private Collection

CATALOGUE 22

Often made in pairs, card tables were clearly a status symbol in federal America. Those who could afford to do so purchased them together for use in homes of higher social and economic standing. Today it is rare for matching pairs to survive together. Without the signature on one of these elegant card tables which, remarkably, were acquired separately and reunited by the current owner, they would be attributed to Boston rather than the Upper Connecticut Valley. Card tables with both serpentine shaped front and side rails were a favorite of John and Thomas Seymour, based on the number of surviving examples.[1] The concentric half-circle lunettes with shaded edging on banding framing the table top edge found here are a hallmark of the work of the Seymour master craftsmen.[2] The effect is created by scorching edges of light wood veneers in hot sand to achieve subtle gradations of brown color (tint).[3] Eastman advertised as a cabinetmaker in Walpole, New Hampshire, in 1811–12 before announcing in 1815 that he has "lately commenced the Cabinet-Making Business in the shop formerly occupied by Mr. Tinney, one door south of Hall's Store, Brattleborough Village." Apparently his Vermont business endeavors were successful, since he advertised several months later for a journeyman chairmaker at this same location.[4]

Delicate and attenuated, the pair match exactly in all aspects, with tops sourced from the same sequence of mahogany boards to suit the distinguishing taste of the unidentified patron. Eastman carried his craftsmanship skills and familiarity with top-of-the-line urban design into the Green Mountain State, although no other documented examples of his work are known to survive.

1. Robert D. Mussey Jr., *The Furniture Masterworks of John & Thomas Seymour* (Salem, MA: Peabody Essex Museum), 347.
2. Mussey, cat. entries 106, 107, 109, 110.
3. Montgomery, 33.
4. Robinson, *Checklist*, 50.

CATALOGUE 23
Card Table, Norwich, Vermont, ca. 1815
Morris Latin Nichols (1794–1870), Merrimack, New Hampshire,
and Norwich, Vermont
Inscription: Written in chalk under bottom: "M.L. Nichols/Norwich"
H. 28 ¼ x W. 35 ¾ x D. 17 ½ inches
Yellow birch, mahogany and birch veneers, eastern white pine
Private Collection

CATALOGUE 23

Morris Nichols had a long career as a chairmaker, first serving his apprenticeship with his brothers-in-law Benjamin Damon (1783–1872) and William Low (1779–1847) in Concord, New Hampshire, where they were in business from 1806 to 1826.[1] At some point before 1830, when he was recorded as a resident engaged in manufactures & trades, Nichols moved to Norwich, Vermont, where he lived until his death in 1870.[2] According to the *History of Windsor County, Vermont*, Morris Nichols was "a rugged thick-set man, below medium height of benevolent self-sacrificing character and courteous manner."[3] He was working in the trade as an artisan and painter until 1860.[4]

On card tables from rural New Hampshire, patterned inlay typically enlivens the edge of the leaf and borders the stringing on the skirt to accent the horizontal lines and wide stance of the object. The square top with elliptical apron featuring highly figured mahogany and the columnar inlay surmounting the legs reveal Nichols's Concord training.[5]

1. *Plain & Elegant Rich & Common Documented New Hampshire Furniture, 1750–1850* (Concord: New Hampshire Historical Society, 1979), 74–75, 143 and 149. Morris's sisters Sophia and Grace Nichols married Benjamin Damon and William Low in 1811 and 1803 respectively. There are five surviving Damon and Low armchairs from the original 1819 commission for the new State House in Concord.
2. Robinson, *Checklist*, 82.
3. *History of Windsor County, Vermont*, edited by Lewis Cass Aldrich and Frank R. Holmes (Vermont: D. Mason and Company, 1891), 498.
4. Robinson, *Checklist*, 82.
5. Benjamin Hewitt, "Regional Characteristics of Inlay on American Federal Card Tables," *Antiques,* May, 1982, 1168, plate IV. Card Table made by Levi Bartlett, Concord, New Hampshire, 1808–09.

CATALOGUE 24

Card tables with five legs were especially popular in New York City and the Hudson valley, and they undoubtedly influenced design in urban Vermont environments. Five other examples have been identified that combine a rectangular frame fitted with two large drawers on square tapering legs, utilizing primarily local woods like cherry and maple, and these have been attributed to Rutland makers based on history of ownership as well as secondary sources.[1] The two drawers built into the table frame add a practical touch associated with western Vermont.

1. Zogry, 40, and Hosley, 267.

Card Table, possibly western Vermont, ca. 1810
Cherry, maple, mahogany and cherry veneers, eastern white pine, brass
H. 28 ¾ x W. 36 x D. 17 ¾ inches
Private Collection

CATALOGUE 25
Stand, Charlotte, Vermont, ca. 1815
Attributed to Lemuel Bishop (b. 1788)
Cherry, eastern white pine, basswood, mixed wood inlays, and brass
H. 27 ⅞ x W. 19 ¾ x D. 17 ⅜ inches
Shelburne Museum, 2013–4

CATALOGUE 25, 26, AND 27

Lemuel Bishop was born in Bennington County, Vermont, in 1788 and appears on the census first in Shelburne (1810) and ten years later in Charlotte.[1] Although it is not known where he learned the trade, he was among the first generation of native-born Vermonters to practice cabinetmaking.

Based on the documentation provided by the paper label, it is possible to attribute two related stands to Lemuel Bishop. Distinctive inlaid motifs include a combination of some of the following features: light fan inlays of birch on drawer corners, some with dark wavy ribs created by scorching which are reminiscent of furniture made in Windsor County (see Cat. 17, 18, and 19); contrasting oval inlay on the center of the drawer and the table top, sometimes accompanied by patterned geometric stringing on visible edges and drawer faces; dark lozenge-shaped inlay surmounting pendant icicles on legs found on some Massachusetts, Connecticut, and Rhode Island work; and decorated cuffs ranging from simple scribe lines on the front of the leg only to patterned piecing on three visible sides. The three examples pictured here represent "good" (see Cat. 25), "better" (see Cat. 26), and "best" (see Cat. 27) iterations of the same basic form.

The absence of ornament is a good tactic for saving money on the part of the frugal customer. While no advertisements of Lemuel Bishop have come to light, Luther Ames of Guilford offered the following in the *Federal Galaxy"* in 1797: "tables of various kinds, candle-stands . . . The above work will be enriched with carving or inlaying, if required"[2] — clearly for additional cost.

A double drop-leaf Pembroke table was sold at William Smith Auctions, Plainfield, New Hampshire, in September 2011, with the identical inlay pattern as the signed stand at Colonial Williamsburg (see Cat. 27) including the addition of the barber-pole banding encircling the drawer fronts. The tantalizing but partially illegible chalk inscription underneath the drawer reads in part, "I will pay you/money that is due/ ? ? of Christ/J...."

---

1. Zogry, fig. 25.
2. Robinson, *Checklist* 29.

CATALOGUE 26
Stand, Charlotte, Vermont, ca. 1815
Attributed to Lemuel Bishop (b. 1788)
Cherry, birch (?), and mahogany inlays, basswood, and brass
H. 27 ½ x W. 18 ¼ x D. 14 ½ inches
Private Collection

CATALOGUE 27

Stand, Charlotte, Vermont, 1815
Lemuel Bishop (b. 1788)
Inscription: Hand-inked paper label on bottom of drawer
"Made by/Lemuel Bishop/Charlotte/1815"
Cherry, birch, pine, with mahogany and birch veneers and light
and dark wood inlays, bone or ivory
H. 27 ½ x W. 21 ¼ x D. 17 ½ inches
The Colonial Williamsburg Foundation, Museum Purchase,
1994-161

CATALOGUE 28B
Detail, P. Carvey Bureau, showing fan inlay,
bone keyhole inlay, and stamped brasses.

CATALOGUE 28

A combination of written documentation and stylistic observations provides mixed messages regarding the origins of this piece of furniture. Although it is stamped with the name of a Bennington resident listed in the 1820 census, suggesting a southern Vermont provenance,[1] this bureau exhibits distinct characteristics associated with other regions. The inlaid corner fans of light and dark wood are found in Windsor County, the central drop panel is suggestive of New Hampshire work,[2] and the dramatic ogee scrolled base suggests Massachusetts.[3] The hardware and escutcheons bear further comment. The oval brasses stamped with an eagle and "U.S.A. E Pluribus Unum" and the diamond-shaped bone keyhole inlay on only the top four drawers (see Cat. 28B) are not usually found on Vermont furniture, but are more characteristic of high-style urban craftsmanship.[4] The five- rather than standard four-drawer layout suggests that this bureau was a special commission. One can only speculate whether the unidentified F. Fisher was a subsequent owner who relocated elsewhere in the country and had the bureau shipped to him from the Stonewall shop in Boston or returned to him there.

1. Peter Carvey is listed in the United States Federal Census, 1820 in Bennington. He also served as a private in the War of 1812 "United States Registers of Enlistments in the U.S. Army, 1798–1914," index and images, *FamilySearch* (https://familysearch.org/pal:/MM9.1.1/QJD5-JCZV : accessed 31 Oct 2014), Peter Carvey, 1813.
2. Brock Jobe, ed., *Portsmouth Furniture: Masterworks from the New Hampshire Seacoast*, figs. 11–13.
3. Zogry, fig. 12.
4. Mussey, cat. entries 49 and 54.

Bureau, 1815
P. Carvey, Bennington, Vermont
Inscription: Branded inside under top: "P. Carvey"
Paper shipping label on back: "Stonewall, Boston, F. Fisher"
Cherry, cherry veneer, bone inlay, eastern white pine, brass
H. 45 ½ x W. 41 ½ x D. 20 inches
Private Collection

CATALOGUE 29
Stand, central Vermont, 1820
Albert Corbin
Inscribed: "This stand was made by Albert Corbin for Nehemiah Pepper prior to 1828"
Cherry, mahogany veneer, eastern white pine, basswood, brass
H. 28 x W. 18 ½ x D. 18 ½ inches
Private Collection

CATALOGUE 29

The clean (elegant but plain) appearance of some early nineteenth-century furniture was an intentional accent in neoclassical homes in early Vermont. The inscription on this four-legged stand, a generic form found throughout the Connecticut River valley, provides a tantalizing clue to both the craftsman and customer. While Albert Corbin does not appear in Robinson's *Checklist of Cabinetmakers,* both surnames Corbin and Pepper are found in Central Vermont records.[1] Although it is not yet possible to pinpoint the stand's place of origin, the positioning of the geometric inlays (in this case five diamonds) and contrasting surrounding string inlay on the top surface are not uncommon on small tables in the Green Mountain State (see Cat. 27 and 32.)

1. U.S. 1810 Census: Corbins were found in: Putney, Wardsboro, Berlin, Norwich, Middlebury, Lincoln, and Grafton. Peppers were found in: Washington, Orwell, and Paulet. U.S. 1820 Census: Corbins were found in Randolph, Middlebury, Royalton, Craftsbury, and Grand Isle. Peppers were found in Washington, Orwell, and Paulet.

CATALOGUE 30

This elegant corner washstand—a form popular in urban centers such as Boston and the North Shore of Massachusetts, is derived from the "Bason Stand," shown in plate 83 in George Hepplewhite's 1794 *Cabinet-Maker and Upholsterer's Guide*.[1] It is fitted with an aperture at the top to accept a basin and a shelf below to hold a pitcher of water.

This is the only documented piece of furniture attributed to Horace Nichols of Middlebury. According to the contemporary record of ownership recorded in pencil on the back of the drawer, "This stand [was made] by H. Nichols for my grandmother Jean who lived in Addison Co. She died in the 1840s or 1850s. This stand was given to my mother in 1897 and then [to] me after her death. R. Jewell."

Nichols's long career began in 1813 and is well documented in local newspaper advertisements from 1817 until his death in 1849.[2] In 1818 Hastings Warren (1799–1845) turned over his prolific cabinetmaker operations to Nichols until 1838. Nichols built "a large assortment of cabinet furniture, such as Secretaries, Bureaus, Book Cases, Ward Robes, Tables, Fancy Work, Light, and Wash Stands, High Post, French, Cot and Turn-up Bed Steads, Sofas, Bed Sofas and chairs."

---

1. George Hepplewhite, *Cabinet-Maker and Upholsterer's Guide* (New York: Dover, 1959), pl. 83.
2. Robinson, *Checklist*, 82.

Washstand, 1820
Horace Nichols (1788–1849), Middlebury, Vermont
Cherry, eastern white pine with cherry, mahogany, and maple veneers
H. 43 ¾ x W. 25 ¾ x D. 18 inches
Shelburne Museum, 1996–1

CATALOGUE 31
Stand, ca. 1815
Cavendish, Vermont
Cherry, mahogany veneer, brass catch
H. 27 x W. 15 ⅞ x D. 16 inches
Shelburne Museum, 1998.83-1

CATALOGUE 32
Stand, ca. 1815
Cavendish, Vermont
Cherry, mahogany veneer
H. 28 x W. 18 ¾ x D. 18 ¼ inches
Private Collection

CATALOGUE 31 AND 32

The documentation on this remarkable tilt-top stand (see Cat. 31) provides the origin for two additional pieces by an unidentified Cavendish, Vermont, cabinetmaking shop. The handwritten inscription in ink on paper attached underneath the top reads:

"All the wood of which this table consists is from 4 cherry stones brought from Ashby [Massachusetts] by Sarah wife of Salmon Dutton Esq. in 1781 the time they moved to Cavendish it being the 37th of his and 34th of hir age and by hir planted near their house of which many bushels of cherrys have been collected and 1815 cut down and sawed and finished and this table was made together with 3 more 3 of which they gave to their children each of them one."

The documented table has a square two-board cherry surface with ovolo corners and no inlay. It descended continuously in the Dutton family and in 1998 was returned to its place of origin: the 1782 Dutton house from Cavendish which Shelburne Museum founder Electra Havemeyer Webb relocated to the grounds in 1950 as the first structure brought to the property. The original Salmon Dutton (1743–1824) constructed the saltbox house as his family residence and place of business. He owned a toll road, worked as a road surveyor, and served the town as selectman, justice of the peace, and surveyor. His descendants who occupied the house until 1900 added wings that served as a store and inn and provided housing for mill workers.

Distinguishing characteristics on two surviving examples include highly arched tripod legs placed in a wide stance that terminate in elongated spade "ballerina" feet that appear to be set "on point"; and a disproportionately short, turned pillar for the table's overall height of approximately 27 inches. The second related table, pictured here (see Cat. 32), features a square fixed top with a fylfot mahogany inlay (four-lobed pinwheel with rounded arms) in the center. A third table has recently emerged in a private collection with a closely related turned column and a two-board cherry octagonal tilt top with string inlay on the edge.[1]

---

1. Letter in object file, 3.6-157, Shelburne Museum.

CATALOGUE 33

Very little is documented regarding cabinetmaking traditions in Berlin, Vermont, where the business seems to have been dominated by the Dewey family. Daniel Dewey learned his trade in the shop of his father, Israel (1777–1862), a native of Hanover, New Hampshire, who became a resident of Berlin in 1801, the year his son was born. Daniel practiced his trade here until November 25, 1825, when he announced that he was relocating to Northfield to carry on his business of selling "Plain and Elegant Furniture" and advertised the need to hire a journeyman cabinetmaker. At the same time he urged his delinquent Berlin customers to "make settlement" in person or, if a second call was necessary, by deputy by January 5, 1826.[1] Though he was clearly a better cabinetmaker than businessman, his bureau represents a universally popular form inspired in part by published patterns that appeared in George Hepplewhite's *Cabinet-Maker and Upholsterer's Guide*.[2] The piece is distinguished by the selection of contrasting native woods and the unusual pigeon-toed rather than flaring French feet. The unusual foot profile is reminiscent of the identified work of rural cabinetmaker Nathan Lombard (1777–1847) of Sutton, Massachusetts. Raised in Brimfield, Massachusetts, Lombard eventually settled in 1805 in nearby Sutton, where he practiced his craft and produced chests and desks best known for his masterful use of intricate pictorial inlay (eagles, vines, and flowers) for his sophisticated clientele.[3]

1. Robinson, *Checklist*, 47.
2. Hepplewhite, Dover, pl. 83.
3. Brock Jobe and Clark Pearce, "Sophistication in Rural Massachusetts: The Inlaid Cherry Furniture of Nathan Lombard," *American Furniture* (Milwaukee: The Chipstone Foundation, 1998), 164–96.

CATALOGUE 33
Bureau, 1821, Berlin, Vermont
Daniel H. Dewey (1801–73), Berlin, Vermont
Inscribed: In black ink on back, "1821 Berlin VT Daniel Dewey"
and in red crayon inside second drawer
Yellow birch, maple and mahogany veneer, basswood, brass
H. 38 ⅛ x W. 41 ¼ x D. 18 ⅛ inches
Private Collection

CATALOGUE 34B
Detail, Aaron Miltimore Bureau, showing
inscription written in red chalk on underside
of bonnet drawer: "Aaron Miltimore/Weston
Vermont."

CATALOGUE 34

This cherry chest with highly stylized acanthus carving and rope-turned
legs is the only known work bearing the signature of Aaron Miltimore.
He was born in Londonderry, New Hampshire, baptized in Windsor,
Vermont, and raised in Windham, Vermont. He married Polly Bridge
(1805–74) from Weston in 1827, and perhaps this chest was made on the
occasion of their wedding to celebrate their nuptials.[1]

While no documents have surfaced indicating that Miltimore was
a cabinetmaker, the red chalk used in the name inscription is also
evident throughout the chest in calculations and measurement mark-
ings. A washstand labeled by Lyman Briggs (b. 1803) of Montpelier,
Vermont, survives with nearly identical carving.[2] Perhaps Miltimore
trained with Briggs when the latter advertised for "two or three jour-
neymen cabinetmakers and an apprentice" early in 1826.[3]

Miltimore had left Vermont by 1839 and became one of the original settlers of Avon Township in Illinois, where he was known as a
farmer. He is buried in the Avon Center cemetery.[4]

1. Erik Gronning, "Discovery," *Antiques & Fine Art*, Summer 3, no. 3 (2002), 18.
2. Zogry, fig. 87.
3. Robinson, *Checklist*, 37.
4. Gronning.

CATALOGUE 34
Bureau, Weston, Vermont, 1827
Aaron Fitz Miltimore (1801–52)
Inscribed: Written in red chalk on bottom of bonnet drawer:
"Aaron Miltimore/Weston Vermont"
Cherry, eastern white pine, and brass
H. 50 ¼ x W. 42 ½ x D. 19 ¼ inches
Vermont Historical Society, 2005.45

CATALOGUE 35
Bureau, Middlebury, Vermont, late 1820s
Basswood, mahogany veneer, brass (replaced)
H. 53 ½ x W. 47 x D. 24 inches
Shelburne Museum, 2014-14

CATALOGUE 35B
Detail, Middlebury Bureau, showing carved basket.

CATALOGUE 35

This bureau, with its carved basket of flowers centered on the shaped splashboard, is one of the few examples of Vermont furniture decorated with relief carving that recalls the work of Salem, Massachusetts, craftsman Samuel McIntyre (1757–1811).[1] The six-lobed flowers and veined leaves surrounded by melons create a three-dimensional representation of a still-life painting. Watermelons appear frequently as subjects in theorems produced with the aid of stencils[2] as well as on the back splats of Hitchcock chairs dating from the 1830s. This bouquet is almost invisibly applied to the bureau's backsplash and is nearly identical to its counterpart, a similar bureau with a strong Middlebury provenance that displays a silhouetted basket probably carved by the same unidentified artist.[3] The punched backgrounds on both baskets are similar and relate to the tooled work found on the Middlebury sofa attributed to Nahum Parker (see Cat. 39). The two bureaus also share similarly executed rope-turned columns topped by a stylized pineapple—elements that suggest the same local cabinetmaking tradition. Unfortunately the paper label attached to the underside of the bottom drawer potentially identifying the maker has been removed.

The appearance of the glove boxes seen in this example is anticipated by Shaftsbury cabinetmaker James Howlet, who advertised in 1824 "Three Elegant Mahogany Bureaus, with drawers on the top. Cash price, $22.00."[4] The increasing rhythm of one, two, and three horizontal sets of drawers, punctuated by brass hardware, progressing up the front of the case, combined with the receding and advancing facade with central blocking, is carefully orchestrated. The resulting mass and movement create a case that is visually never at rest.

1. Montgomery, fig. 264.
2. Richard Miller, *A Shared Legacy Folk Art in America* (Alexandria, VA: Art Services International; New York: Skira Rizzoli Publications, Inc., 2014), 136–37.
3. Zogry, fig. 43.
4. Robinson, *Checklist,* 66, and Zachariah Harwood's description of the small drawers on top of his curly maple bureau, "Rich and Tasty: Vermont Furniture to 1850," p. 30.

CATALOGUE 36

In 1825 Lyman Briggs established a furniture warehouse on State Street in Vermont's capital city, where he remained in business until 1846.[1] His 1830 advertisements in the *Vermont Watchman* indicate his familiarity with the latest styles in cabinet furniture in New York, Boston, and London, which he brought to his rural customers.[2] He sold furniture wholesale and retail and was a conduit for the transmission of design from urban areas. This Grecian Pembroke table, which descended in the Hubbard family of Montpelier,[3] exhibits late neoclassical cabinetwork in the lyre pedestal and robust carved feet punctuated by carved sunflower bosses (see Cat. 36B).

1. Jason T. Busch, "The Briggs Family Business and Furniture: A Study of Patronage and Consumption in Antebellum Southwestern New Hampshire," *Rural New England Furniture: People, Place, and Production*, The Dublin Seminar for New England Folklife Annual Proceedings 1998 (Boston: Boston University, 1998), 138–156, 148.
2. Robinson, *Checklist*, 37.
3. Zogry, 143.

CATALOGUE 36B
Detail, Lyman Briggs table, showing lyre pedestal.

Drop-Leaf Pedestal-Base Table, Montpelier, ca. 1825
Attributed to Lyman Briggs (b. 1803)
Mahogany and white pine
H. 28 ½ x W. 24 (with leaves down) x D. 42 inches
Vermont Historical Society, 45.193

CATALOGUE 37

The monumental secretary by Hastings Warren (see Cat. 37), with its imposing cornice, arched pediment, convex façade, and veneered, figured mahogany surfaces framed with cross banding, is similar to designs produced by J. W. Meeks in New York City (see Fig. 37B). Both pieces feature turned columns with carved Ionic capitals which also appear prominently on the signed sideboard bookcase (see Cat. 43) from Randolph, Vermont, dated 1829.

In addition, the Hastings Warren secretary anticipates the Gothic revival style in the pointed arches enclosing spiky fretwork found on the glazed doors—elements which originally decorated medieval castles rather than furniture. As Bill Hosley has pointed out, this fashionable feature was perhaps inspired by the Gothic revival church built in Middlebury in 1826, the first of its design in the state of Vermont.[1] In 1805 Hastings Warren established his cabinet and chair-making business in Middlebury, where he advertised "the following articles of furniture, viz. Sofas, Side-boards, Secretaries Book-cases, Desks, Bureaus, Tables, Chests. High-Post, Field, French, & Plain bedsteads. Fancy, Work, Wash & Light Stands. Also 500 well made Chairs, consisting of Fancy, Armed, Rocking, Dining & Children's Chairs." He practiced the trade until 1834, when the Sheriff of Middlebury advertised in the *Middlebury Free Press* an auction sale "at General H. Warren's Cabinet shop . . . Seven Hundred Dollars worth of cabinet Furniture, of the best kind and newest fashions."[2]

1. Hosley, 279.
2. Robinson, *Checklist*, 106-107.

FIGURE 37B
Secretary Bookcase, New York, ca. 1835
Attributed to Joseph Meeks (1771–1868)
H. 97 x W. 48 x D. 25 inches
Mahogany
Photo courtesy Cottone Auctions, Geneseo, NY

Secretary, Middlebury, Vermont, ca. 1830
Hastings Warren (1779–1845)
Inscription: Signed in pencil on a drawer bottom: "H. Warren"
Mahogany, cherry, and eastern white pine with mahogany and birch veneers
H. 92 ½ x W. 55 x D. 23 inches
Sheldon Museum

CATALOGUE 38
Secretary, central Vermont, ca. 1830
Cherry, mahogany veneers, eastern white pine, and brass
H. 63 ½ (70 with pediment) x W. 40 x D. 18 ½ inches
Collection of J. Brooks Buxton

CATALOGUE 38

This secretary has descended continuously in the family of the current owner's great-great-grandfather Freeman Buxton (1804–86), who resided on Buxton Farm in Marshfield, Vermont. It is closely related in form and materials to another secretary published with a history of belonging to Libbeus Bennett of Northfield.[1] They both share arched glazed doors, rope-turned legs and carefully bookmatched mahogany veneers. The only difference in layout is the use of three long horizontal drawers in the lower case of the Northfield example.

The central plinth within this scrolled pediment was never drilled to receive a finial, a curious feature also found on the Otis Warren bureau (see Cat. 70) and the Oramel Partridge sideboard/bookcase (see Cat. 43).

1. Hosley, 277.

CATALOGUE 38B
Central Vermont Secretary, closed.

CATALOGUE 39
Sofa, ca. 1830, Middlebury, Vermont
Attributed to Nahum Parker (1789–1876)
Mahogany, white pine, and mahogany veneer, brass
H. 35 x W. 84 x D. 20 ½ inches
Collection of J. Brooks Buxton

CATALOGUE 39

The lyre design was a popular component of the Greek revival style of the 1820s and 1830s and is found in a variety of furniture forms including table supports (see Cat. 36) and chair splats (see Cat. 24). Here, the maker incorporates the entire face and facade of a lyre clock in the arm supports of this sofa. The quality and quantity of the high relief carving on the legs and leg supports is exceptional, and its placement on front, back (see Cat. 39C), and side surfaces suggests that this impressive seating unit was meant to hold court in the center of a parlor. The star-punched backgrounds (see Cat. 39C) in particular relate to Boston-area practice. Although it is unsigned, the sofa's attribution to Nahum Parker is based on the survival of three additional sofas with the lyre device, one at the Sheldon Museum in Middlebury. The current upholstery is not original,[1] but the gilded metal strip framing the edges is also found on the Sheldon example. Existing receipts indicate that Parker purchased "St. Domingo Mahogany plank" from Boston and horsehair cloth from a New York supplier.[2] In an 1829 advertisement in the *National Standard*, Nahum Parker specifically publicized that he had on hand "two Sofas, trimmed in elegant style."[3] Could this be one of them? Upholstered sofas requiring specialized skills were one of the most expensive furniture forms in New England households during the 1830s.[4]

1. The sofa was reupholstered in the period "Napoleon Bee" pattern reproduced in 54-inch widths. The original fabric would have been created on narrower looms measuring 24–30 inches wide, resulting in more seams.
2. Bill of sale of Benjamin Lamson to Nahum Parker, October 1, 1828, and bill of sale of Thorpe to Nahum Parker, April 25, 1840, Sheldon Museum archives.
3. Robinson, *Checklist*, 85.
4. Hosley, *Old-Time New England,* 72:259 (1987), 283.

CATALOGUE 39B
Detail, Nahum Parker Sofa, showing lyre-shaped arm support.

CATALOGUE 39C
Detail, Nahum Parker Sofa, showing star-punched background on rear of feet.

A Distinctively Vermont Form

CATALOGUE 40

Fully-developed federal sideboards (see Cat. 17, 58, and 59) are not common in Vermont, although they were frequently advertised by cabinetmakers. Instead, a smaller modification of this form—combining a bureau with flanking bottle drawers—survives in many areas of the Green Mountain State. Stylistically, this refined new hybrid that Vermont cabinetmakers in the 1830s advertised as either a half sideboard or locker[1] features a mixture of highly figured native woods (bookmatched cherry panels and tiger maple) combined with more expensive veneers (mahogany and rosewood veneers). The blocked front and exuberantly spool-turned corner columns, combined with the vigorously scrolled apron, add to the cabinetmakers' eccentric interpretations of this high-style piece. According to very specific written documentation, this half sideboard was made by Ebenezer Wheeler for Sarah Smith (1786–1866) on the occasion of her May 6, 1817, marriage[2] to Reverend Isaac B. Bucklen (1794–1875), whose name is inked on the backboards. Little is known about Ebenezer Wheeler, who appears in the 1820 Census for Rockingham, engaged in "Manufactures." Only one other piece of his is known—a signed four-drawer bureau with shaped skirt and similar splashboard, marked Saxtons River and dated 1819.[3]

1. Charles A. Robinson, *Vermont Cabinetmakers & Chairmakers Before 1855: A Checklist* (Shelburne, VT: Shelburne Museum, 1994), see William Alvord, 28, Frederick Coffin, 42, James Howland, 66, Horace Livingston, 75, Samuel Payne, 86.
2. www.bucklindata.net accessed October 28, 2014.
3. *Maine Antiques Digest*, December 1983, 40-b Lippincott antiques.

Half Sideboard, 1817
Ebenezer Wheeler (b. 1791–94), Rockingham, Vermont
Cherry, yellow birch, tiger maple with mahogany, maple,
and rosewood veneers, poplar, and eastern white pine
H. 47 ½ x W. 47 x D. 21 ½ inches
Shelburne Museum, 2013-11

CATALOGUE 41

Very little is known of Dexter Derby, who with his two brothers, Cyrus (1789–1823) and Lemuel (1792–1875), moved with their parents before 1812 from Orford, New Hampshire, to Bridport, Vermont, where they practiced the cabinetmaking trade until mid-century.[1]

This fashionable half sideboard with Grecian splashboard and varied drawer divisions features light and dark contrasting local, figured woods with unusual canted corners on the tiger maple posts finished/fitted with trapezoidal base elements. However, the sparing use of mahogany veneer on the drawer fronts and the replacement of imported wood with grain paint on the splashboard and top reveal a successful attempt to avoid costly materials.

1. Robinson, *Checklist*, 46.

Half Sideboard, 1836
Dexter Derby (1805–75), Bridport, Vermont
Inscription: Signed twice on underside of top "Dexter Derby" and "March 31, 1836"
Cherry, maple, and pine, with mahogany veneer and paint, glass knobs
H. 51 x W. 47 x D. 21 ½ inches
Sheldon Museum

CATALOGUE 42

This half sideboard, or locker, configured like a lady's secretary, descended in the Smith family of Randolph, Vermont, and was recently acquired by the current owner. Sophisticated contrasting figured veneers are combined with elegant three-dimensional elements in the spool-turned and reeded columns on both front and back corners. The unusual feet do not relate to other central Vermont work and are constructed in two pieces using a wedge-shaped inset to create the elongated, melon-shaped form.

CATALOGUE 42B
Central Vermont Half Sideboard, open.

CATALOGUE 42
Half Sideboard with hinged writing surface
Central Vermont, ca. 1820
Cherry, mahogany and bird's-eye veneers,
eastern white pine, and brass
H. 47 ½ x W. 45 x D. 22 inches
Collection of J. Brooks Buxton

Sideboard/Bookcase, Randolph, Vermont, 1829
Oramel Partridge (1799–1868)
Inscription: Written in black ink on proper right side of long drawer:
"Bought from Oramel Partr/idge/in the year 1829 by/Aaron Storrs"
H. 76 x W. 43 x D. 22 ¼ inches
Flame birch, mahogany veneer, basswood, and eastern white pine
Collection of Ethan Merrill

CATALOGUE 43B
Detail, Oramel Partridge Sideboard/Bookcase, showing carving on column and hairy claw foot with toenails.

CATALOGUE 43

This unusual form, combining a glazed-door secretary placed on top of a half sideboard complete with bottle drawers, may be the realization of what one Vermont cabinetmaker advertised in 1810 as a "secretary with side-board front."[1] Massive in size and masterful in execution, this faux frame-and-panel sideboard containing bottle drawers on the bottom and glazed bookcase above would have held a commanding presence in a wealthy client's home.

The bold execution of Oramel Partridge's sideboard/bookcase relies on acanthus applied panels framing the top two drawers (see Cat. 71 and 72), fully round Ionic columns combining leaf and pineapple motifs, and substantial hairy claw feet with toenails (see Cat. 43B). The complex cornice is fitted with a whale's tail scroll board reminiscent of Connecticut work but, as in several other Vermont pieces (see Cat. 38 and 70), the plinths and corner blocks are not drilled for finials. The absence of any functional hardware or decorative brass is surprising considering the probable cost for materials and craftsmanship but may, instead, reflect availability issues.

The maker, Oramel Partridge, born in Norwich, Vermont, learned his trade from Isaac Reed in Randolph, where he opened a cabinet-making shop in 1822 and remained in this town his entire life.[2] This sideboard/bookcase represents his only known surviving work. It was commissioned by Aaron Storrs, who was a charter member of the town of Randolph, Vermont, in 1781,[3] and silently proclaims his status in the community.

1. Robinson, *Checklist*, Daniel Bullard, 38.
2. Robinson, *Checklist*, 85. Oramel Partridge is pictured in Harriet M. Chase and Ron Sanford, *Randolph Vermont 1777–1977: Its Discovery, Creation, and Development* (Randolph: Chase & Sanford, 2006), 53.
3. Chase and Sanford, *Randolph Vermont 1777–1977*, 28. In 1780 "Captain Aaron Storrs has undertaken to build a saw-mill and grist-mill in the township of Randolph and this property granted to two-hundred acres of land in said township." Captain Aaron Storrs, "considered the father of Randolph," is pictured on page 29. The maker, Oramel Partridge, is listed as one of "five sleigh manufacturers at the [town] center," 53.

Vermont Uncorked

CATALOGUE 44

A note accompanying this unusual desk is inscribed "Made in 1859 by Alonzo Stowe, Books painted by Truman Town." The creator may be Alonzo Stowell (1828–98), with the last two letters abraded.[1] He probably learned his cabinetmaking skills from his father, Horace Stowell (1803–78), a resident of Londonderry from 1818 until his death. Horace's successful entrepreneurial activities are recorded in the 1860 industrial census, where H Stowell & Son are listed as cabinetmakers with an annual production of twelve bureaus, thirty tables and stands, and other articles.[2] The connection between Truman Town, occupation unknown, in northwestern Washington County, Vermont, in 1860[3] and the southwestern Vermont Londonderry cabinetmaker suggests the travels of an itinerant house sign and fancy painter.

The totally unexpected feature on this 1830s-style rectangular table with hinged leaf and turned legs ending in peg feet is the unique superstructure featuring carved and painted trompe l'oeil book form drawer fronts. The painted title on the spine of one volume is T. S. Arthur's *True Riches*, published in 1852,[4] confirming the accuracy of the date of the accompanying inscription. Based purely on visual evidence, it is surprising this table was produced as late as mid-century.

---

1. Charles A. Robinson, *Vermont Cabinetmakers & Chairmakers Before 1855: A Checklist* (Shelburne, VT: Shelburne Museum, 1994), 100.
2. Robinson, *Checklist*, 100.
3. Truman Aseph Town, b. 1836, Woodbury, Washington, VT, age 24, United States Federal Census 1860.
4. *True Riches or Wealth without Wings* (Philadelphia: J. W. Bradley, 1852).

Desk/Table, 1852
Made by Alonzo Stowell (1828–98), Londonderry, Vermont
Painted decoration by Truman Town (b. 1836), Washington County, Vermont
Bird's-eye maple and paint
H. 39 x W. 30 x D. 16 inches
Private collection

CATALOGUE 45
Card Table, Burlington, Vermont, 1818
Made by Ebenezer White, Burlington, Vermont
Inscribed in pencil on underside of the drawer : "E. E. White/
Burlington Vt./1818"
Cherry, yellow birch, cherry and mahogany veneers, soft
maple, basswood, sandwich glass knobs
H. 28 ½ x W. 35 ⅞ x D. 17 ½ inches
Private Collection

CATALOGUE 45

Striking in its classical proportions and elegant simplicity, this card table supported on slender tapering legs with distinctive rings at the ankles stands on feet that terminate in small ball turnings. This detail relates to a bow-front chest of drawers inscribed "Jacob Carter Athol Worc[ester] Co." in the collection of Historic Deerfield.[1] Carter (1796–1886) was born in Leominster, Massachusetts, and in 1810 apprenticed to Athol cabinetmaker Alden Spooner (1784–1877) before establishing a shop in Belchertown, Massachusetts, seven years later. The sandwich glass knobs are original.

An Ebenezer White appears as a longtime resident of Burlington, in the 1810 to 1850 censuses, and an E. E. White, probably his son, was in business with Stephen and Joel Gates, furniture and cabinetmakers in Brattleboro in the 1850s.[2] A federal secretary desk of mahogany with bird's-eye maple veneers with the same distinctive feet and signed E. E. White, Brattleboro, Vermont, was recently sold at auction.[3] Although the maker's age and origins are unknown, he was familiar with elements of Connecticut Valley style. The use of a drawer in the table frame is pure Vermont.

1. Historic Deerfield, Inc., 0422.
2. Robinson, *Checklist*, 110.
3. Thomaston Place Auction Galleries, Thomaston, Maine, 21–22 May 2011, lot 115.

CATALOGUE 46

This is the only known work signed by James Richardson, who emigrated in 1816 from Sterling, Massachusetts, to Poultney, Vermont, where he resided until his death. In 1817, he advertised in the *Rutland Herald* that "he has on hand for sale of the latest Boston patterns, Mahogany sideboards, Secretaries, Card Tables, Ladies Work Tables and Wash stands."[1] Clearly the overall form of this worktable and the careful selection of figured woods reflect its fashionable urban origins. However, the execution is outside the envelope. From the undulating backsplash terminating in swirling rosettes, to the serpentine front, turned columnar supports, and C-scroll legs, there is hardly a straight line. This remarkable worktable is clearly not part of Richardson's standard repertoire but was most probably created as a special commission for a discriminating customer and was made to fit comfortably on a pier between two windows for maximum light.

1. Robinson, *Checklist*, 92.

CATALOGUE 46
Worktable, ca. 1825
James Richardson (1794–1861), Poultney, Vermont
Inscribed in pencil in top drawer: "Richardson Poultney"
Maple, mahogany, maple and butternut veneers, yellow birch,
eastern white pine, brass
H. 28 x W. 24 ⅛ x D. 17 inches
Private Collection

CATALOGUE 47
Sideboard with writing interior, Craftsbury, Vermont, 1839
Attributed to Alva J. or Alva Ruggles French (1798–1876),
Craftsbury, Vermont
Cherry, butternut veneer, eastern white pine and basswood,
brass knobs (replaced)
H. 54 ¼ x W. 70 ¼ x D. 22 ½ inches
Collection of Daniel R. Davis

CATALOGUE 47

The hand-written note in this sideboard provides the following detailed information regarding its history:

> This sideboard was made by Mr. (Alva J. or Alva R.) French at Craftsbury Vermont about 1839 for Amory Davison Senior (1790–1867). The price paid for it was $60 and Amory Davison Junior (1830–1906), then a lad of nine years, drew wood from his home to Craftsbury Common to pay for the sideboard. It was given by his grandfather to Amanda Davison (1861–1915) when she was a small girl and was taken by her to Barton, Vermont, in 1885 at the time of her marriage to Harley T. Seaver. She bequeathed it to her daughter Clemma Seaver Root, and it came to her home at her marriage to Edmund M. Root in 1922. In 1930, it was moved to Brattleboro, VT. It was then refinished and new pulls replaced those then in use. (The original pulls were said to have been milk glass. As these became broken they were replaced by ordinary brass ones. These in time were replaced by antique brass reproductions in 1935.) In 1950 it was brought to Burlington by the Roots. It was then given to Barbara Davison Davis in the 1950s and was taken to Cabot, VT. In 2000, it was given to Daniel Robert Davis by his mother Barbara and currently is in Newark, VT. Daniel has bequeathed it to his daughter Beth Davis Seniw and she will be taking possession sometime this year when she moves back to Vermont.

Despite its massive size, this sideboard with hinged fall-front desk has traveled from its origin in the Northeast Kingdom to the southeast, northwest, and back to the northeast corner of the state throughout its long history. Created by Craftsbury native Alva Ruggles French (1798–1876) and/or his nephew Alva J. French (1824–82), who were engaged in Manufactures & Trades under the name A. R. and A. French in 1849,[1] the stylish facade features carefully bookmatched butternut veneers acquired locally, framed by vigorously turned legs and columns topped with acanthus leaf carving (see Cat. 47B). The French family were early settlers in Craftsbury, Vermont, where Samuel French (1766–1864) emigrated from Oakham, Massachusetts, about 1746.[2]

1. Robinson, *Checklist*, 55.
2. Betty Davison Post, *The Founding Families of Craftsbury, Vermont; a study of the relationships between the proprietors and the first settlers of the town* (Lakewood, CO: Bette Davison Post, 2006), 148.

CATALOGUE 47B
Detail, Alva French sideboard, showing butternut veneers and carvings and turnings on columns and legs.

Three Vermont Furniture Puzzles

No study in any aspect of American material culture, including Vermont furniture, is ever complete. New objects and therefore new information and interpretation come to light, while old topics and puzzles remain tough nuts to crack. As we undertook this survey, twenty years after our previous in-depth study of Vermont furniture, three research problems came to mind, all interrelated on the western side of the state along today's U.S. Route 7.

The first puzzle involves the influence of the New York City cabinet shop of the Allison brothers on the Loomis family of cabinetmakers in Shaftsbury, Vermont, and on the work of Hastings Kendrick, also from Shaftsbury. Our second quest focuses on painted furniture by the Matteson family, also of Shaftsbury, and the ways in which the Mattesons chose to interpret high-style furniture in their Vermont town. The final untold tale looks at neoclassical Vermont furniture made in the prosperous towns on the western side of the Green Mountains and asks broader questions about identity and location.

CATALOGUE 48
Bureau, Shaftsbury, Vermont, ca. 1815
Attributed to the Loomis family
Inscribed in pencil under top: "Shafts…"
Maple, maple and mahogany veneers, eastern white pine, brass
H. 45 x W. 43 ½ x D. 19 ¾ inches
Mr. and Mrs. Norman Gronning

THE ALLISON BROTHERS OF NEW YORK AND SHAFTSBURY CRAFTSMEN: CATALOGUE 48

Bureaus made by the Loomis brothers of Shaftsbury, Asa (1793–1868), Daniel (1798–1833), and Russell (1799–1854),[1] are linked in both proportion and construction to urban furniture labeled by Richard Allison (1780–1825), who worked in New York City. One of the brothers might have worked with Allison before returning to Vermont or perhaps someone from Allison's shop moved to the Green Mountain State.

This ca. 1815 bureau (see Cat. 48), attributed to the Loomis family in Shaftsbury, seems especially connected to Richard Allison's work in a bureau made ca. 1810 (see Fig. 48B) that also has astragal mahogany veneer outlining the principal drawer. Similarly, a locker/half sideboard (see Zea Fig. 2, p. 13) by Hastings Kendrick, also from Shaftsbury, seems inspired by this Empire sideboard (see Fig. 48C) made by Richard's older brother, Michael Allison (1773–1855), about 1825, also in New York City.[2]

The influence of the Allison brothers on the New York-style design and execution of case furniture made in Shaftsbury, within the watershed of the Hudson River in southwestern Vermont, exemplifies how the documentary evidence of human relationships sometimes begins with the physical evidence of artifacts.

1. Kenneth Joel Zogry, *The Best the Country Affords: Vermont Furniture, 1765–1850*, Philip Zea, ed. (Bennington, VT: The Bennington Museum, 1995), 42–43; Charles A. Robinson, *Vermont Cabinetmakers & Chairmakers Before 1855: A Checklist* (Shelburne, VT: Shelburne Museum, 1994), 75.
2. John L. Scherer, "Allison Brothers: New York City Cabinetmakers," *Antiques & Fine Art*, http://antiquesandfineart.com/articles/article.cfm?request=300; see also Christie's Auction Catalog, Sale #8840, Lot 509, January 16, 1998.

FIGURE 48B
Bureau, labeled by Richard Allison (1780–1825)
New York City, ca. 1810
Mahogany, mahogany and birch veneers, eastern
white pine, tulip poplar
H. 46 x W. 45 x D. 20 ½ inches
Courtesy of New York State Museum

FIGURE 48C
Sideboard, labeled by Michael Allison (1773–1855)
New York City, ca. 1825
Mahogany, mahogany veneer, eastern white pine, tulip poplar
H. 59 x W. 61 x D. 26 inches
Courtesy of New York State Museum

CATALOGUE 49
Tavern Sign, Bennington, Vermont, ca. 1860
"General Stark of Bennington"/E Noyes
Wood and paint
H. 30 x W. 33 ¾ inches (D. unrecorded)
Shelburne Museum, 27.FT-51

THE SIGN-PAINTING TRADITION

The trade of ornamental painting, like that practiced by the Matteson family in Shaftsbury, has deep roots in the artisanship of early New England. As early as 1647 the Colony of Massachusetts decreed that every establishment "shall have some inoffensive sign, obvious, for the direction of strangers posted within three months of its licensing."[1] Before the spread of literacy, shopkeepers relied on painted symbols to attract business and identify the services that they offered. These eye-catching visual messages contained little text but relied on colorful graphics created by the ornamental painter who, by the 1820s, played an important part in the appearance of free-standing furniture (see Cat. 50, 51, 52, and 53).

Taverns and inns traditionally were named for great historical figures. Revolutionary War icon General John Stark (1728–1822), depicted here, who fought at the Battle of Bennington, August 16, 1775, would have been familiar iconography that alerted passersby that food, drink, and lodging were available within. E. (Eugene) Noyes (b. 1847), whose occupation was listed as stove dealer, owned stores in Hampton, New Hampshire, and Amesbury, Massachusetts, suggesting that he may also have managed an inn or tavern as well in southern Vermont, but no documentation to that effect has been found.[2]

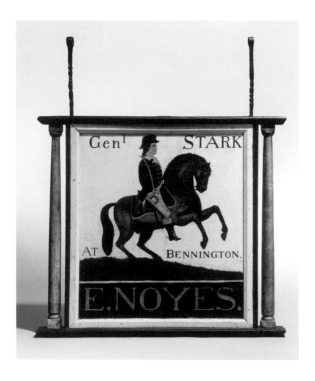

125

1. www.nationalheritagemuseum.org/.../ByTheWay." Accessed December 13, 2014.
2. *A Bountiful Plenty at Shelburne Museum: Folk Art Traditions in America* (Shelburne, VT: Shelburne Museum, 2000). Traveling exhibition organized by the Trust for Museum Exhibitions. https://speedweb.speedmuseum.org/Docent%20Web/labels%20exhibitions/shelburne1.htm. Accessed December 20, 2014.

CATALOGUE 50
Chest over Two Drawers
Probably Shaftsbury, Vermont, ca. 1815
Painted eastern white pine
H. 36 ¼ x W. 36 ¼ x D. 16 ¼ inches
Shelburne Museum, 1959-281

PAINTED FURNITURE BY THE MATTESON FAMILY:
CATALOGUE 50, 51, 52, AND 53

The second unsolved mystery is the furniture ascribed to the Matteson family, also in Shaftsbury.[1] (The chest pictured as Cat. 51 bears the Matteson inscription.) The furniture is as famous as any made in Vermont for its use of ornamental paint to simulate vibrant hardwood veneers. But who really were the various members of the Matteson family? More importantly, who among them were cabinetmakers and/or ornamental painters? And for that matter, what, if any, were the relationships between the Loomises and the Mattesons, not to mention Hastings Kendrick, in this single Vermont town?

High-style urban furniture was skillfully imitated in both urban and rural areas using more readily available and affordable materials to reach a broader clientele. Itinerant ornamental painters in Vermont and northern New England plied their trade with pine and paint on both furniture, architecture, and signage (see Cat. 49) to create realistically grained exotic hardwoods in the latest fashion. Many craftsmen practiced these skills, explaining the widely different painting styles on the furniture once attributed solely to the Matteson family. For example, Bristol cabinetmaker Kendrick Follet (1802–61) advertised in the *Middlebury Argus* in 1833 that he had on hand "a fine assortment of stained and painted [chairs and settees in] imitation of Rose Wood."[2]

Most of these lift-top blanket boxes and chests are similar in form and decorative concept and probably date between 1815 and 1825, with the exception of the 1803 example made a generation earlier (see Cat. 51). In all of this furniture, the ornamental paint is conceptualized as if it were hardwood veneer except that the painted medium allows for exaggeration in both size and graphic impact, making paint in a way better than wood. For example, Catalogue 52 and 53 share a fancifully grained front panel (either oval- or astragal- shaped) surrounded by a band of solid color (red or blue or grain-painted to simulate cross-banding), which is often repeated on the sides (see Cat. 52). Both the lid and the back of the Harwood Painted Chest (see Cat. 53) reiterate the oval motif, which is surrounded by a realistically tiger-grained border, on all five visible surfaces. The chest is designed for viewing on all sides, perhaps at home or just as likely as a traveling trunk. The handwritten inscription on the bottom is a shipping label to a customer in Hartford, Connecticut, confirming that these faux-grained containers traveled beyond Vermont.[3]

CATALOGUE 51
Chest over Two Drawers
Inscribed: "Made By J. Matteson August 1 A.D. 1803"
Probably Shaftsbury, Vermont, 1803
Painted eastern white pine
H. 40 x W. 46 ½ x D. 20 ¼ inches
Historic Deerfield, Inc., 1979.100
Museum purchase with funds donated by
Mr. and Mrs. Gregory M. Cook

Chest
Probably Shaftsbury, Vermont, ca. 1825
Painted yellow poplar
H. 24 ½ x W. 46 x D. 18 ⅜ inches
Collections of Old Sturbridge Village, Sturbridge,
Massachusettts, 5.7.160

CATALOGUE 53B
Detail, Chest, probably Shaftsbury, Vermont, ca. 1825, showing inscription "E Harwood/Hartford/Conn." in black paint on the bottom.

These variations in painting styles are also explained within the Matteson family by the different names (and spellings) inscribed on five chests: "By J. Matteson/August 1 A.D. 1803" [Historic Deerfield]; "Thomas G. Matison/South Shaftsbury/V.t." [Henry Ford Museum, destroyed 1970]; "Thomas Matteson/S Shaftsbury, Vermont, 1824" [Henry Ford Museum]; "W.[?] P. Matteson/S. Shaftsbury" [Private Collection]; and "Benonia Matteson to B. Burlingame Dr. [debit]/To paint $2.70/To Paint & Grain Chest $2.00/$4.70" [Private Collection]. Beyond simple ownership, the first inscription connotes that the construction and/or the painting of the chest was performed by a "J. Matteson" (see Cat. 51), while the last significantly shows that at least one of the Mattesons was in fact an ornamental painter.

The probability is that non-Matteson family cabinetmakers also worked in this medium and that their work may have been painted by Mattesons or by other ornamental painters. For example, a painted basswood bureau (see Cat. 54), sold by Skinner Auctions in 1999, is closely related to this group and is inscribed: "Henry Davist . . . Readsboro [Vermont] Feb . . . 1815 $7.50."[4] The reality and working hypothesis is that in probability this case furniture—hardwood and painted—was made in the Shaftsbury area by interrelated craftsmen, perhaps competitors but quite possibly the same broad shop tradition working to develop a wider range of wares for their Bennington County clientele.

1. Caroline Hebb, "A Distinctive Group of Early Vermont Furniture," *The Magazine Antiques* 104, no. 4 (October 1973): 458–461; Zogry, 46; David Krashes, "The South Shaftsbury, Vermont, Painted Wooden Chests," *Rural New England Furniture: People, Place, and Production*. Proceedings of the Dublin Seminar for New England Folklife (Boston: Boston University, 1998): 226–235. Furniture associated with the Matteson family in public collections includes examples at Henry Ford Museum, Historic Deerfield, Museum of American Folk Art, Old Sturbridge Village, and Shelburne Museum.
2. Robinson, *Checklist*, 54.
3. The 1830 United States Federal census lists Ebenezer Harwood in Stafford, Tolland County, Connecticut, which is 30 miles north of Hartford. The remnant of bright blue paint is most likely a pigment check to evaluate the final appearance of the color on raw wood.
4. Skinner Auction Catalog, Sale # 1902, February 28, 1999, Lot 211. The location of the bureau is unknown to the authors. Readsboro and Shaftsbury are thirty miles apart in southern Vermont. Daviston or Davidson is not listed in Robinson, *Checklist*.

Chest
Probably Shaftsbury, Vermont, ca. 1825
Inscription: "E. Harwood/Hartford/Conn" in black
paint on the bottom
Painted eastern white pine
H. 24 ½ x W. 42 ¼ x D. 19 inches
Private Collection

The final untold tale is central to understanding neoclassical Vermont furniture on the western side of the Green Mountains and should be analyzed in context more closely with the Loomis-Matteson furniture. The questions here are more broadly about identity and location: Who are the craftsmen behind the wildly veneered, quintessential Vermont bureaus and secretaries that the painted Shaftsbury-related furniture emulates? And where were they? Until further notice, it seems reasonable to back away from specific attributions to Rutland, Middlebury, and Burlington until more firmly documented furniture is identified. The truth is that we just do not know for certain who made this furniture or specifically where, although circumstantial evidence points to Middlebury as the veneer capital of Vermont.

The furniture itself is usually supported on French feet and is characterized by highly figured, "curl'd" and bird's-eye maple veneers and skirts with dramatic ogee curves often flanking a rectangular dropped tablet (see Cat. 56B). The latter is inspired by case furniture often associated with Portsmouth, New Hampshire, and southern Maine, suggesting that an unidentified cabinetmaker may have come to western Vermont from that region. The placement of the eye-catching flame birch frieze (seen on Cat. 55 and 57) is distinctive in Vermont furniture and a conscious design choice that gives the design an architectural flair. Astragal-shaped panels in contrasting wood, or rectangular panels with a cross-banded border on each drawer front, differentiate the two basic designs found in the work of these competitive shop traditions. The latter case furniture is sometimes highlighted with an inlaid lozenge motif and is overall more attenuated in design (see Cat. 56B).

Some examples (see Cat. 57) have engaged columns, ovolo corners, and slender turned legs also popular in coastal New England during the first quarter of the nineteenth century.[1] The emphasis here is on the careful selection of dramatic woods like figured bird's-eye maple (drawer facades) and tiger maple (turned elements) placed perfectly to achieve visual balance and movement that never stops.

Looking at this problem of attribution another way, and remembering our introductory "primer" on Vermont furniture connoisseurship that included the Workmanship of Economics, we ask: Which were the more prosperous Vermont towns in Rutland, Addison, and Chittenden counties whose citizens might support craftsmen able to make such aggressive and expensive furniture? Population is not the primary quotient, but there is a clear correlation between the prosperous towns, waterpower and industry, civic growth especially in

1. For example, see Jobe, fig. 14.

Bureau, western Vermont, ca. 1810
Cherry, tiger and bird's-eye maple, and mahogany veneers,
eastern white pine, brass
H. 41 ½ x W. 42 ½ x D. 20 ½ inches
Private Collection

CATALOGUE 55
Bureau, western Vermont, ca. 1810
Maple, cherry, birch, basswood with maple and mahogany
veneers and light and dark wood inlays, brass
H. 41 ⅝ x W. 43 ½ x D. 20 ¼ inches
Private Collection

schools, and extant neoclassical architecture of merit that also clearly housed patrons for expensive, modern furniture. By process of elimination this furniture was probably made in the neighborhood of Rutland and Middlebury, which are a little over thirty miles apart. But what was made in Burlington, which is another thirty-plus miles north of Middlebury and which by mid-century was the largest and wealthiest city in the state?

While we do not know for certain which furniture came from where, the prosperous towns in western Vermont, south to north, in this period were Bennington, Castleton, Rutland, Brandon, Middlebury, and Burlington. Of these, Castleton is noteworthy for the founding of the Castleton Medical College in 1818, the architecture of Thomas Dake (1785–1852), and nearby slate and marble quarries. Rutland is still known for its quarries and was home to cabinetmakers William Hale (1767–1809) and the firm of John P. Clough (born ca. 1791) and William Alvord (1766–1853), whose newspaper advertisements suggest their significance. The wealth of Brandon was keyed to cast iron. Its principal cabinetmaker was Caleb Knowlton (b. 1778), who came to Vermont from Manchester, Massachusetts.

Middlebury was distinguished for its college, established in 1800; its architecture, highlighted by the 1809 meetinghouse by Lavius Fillmore (1767–1850) constructed at a cost of $9000; and its quarried vein of black marble that can be seen in part from the bridge at the falls on Otter Creek in the middle of town. By 1830 Middlebury was the second largest town in the state. Its principal cabinetmakers were Horace Nichols (1788–1849) from Litchfield, Connecticut, Nahum Parker (1789–1876) from Stoddard, New Hampshire, and Hastings Warren (1779–1845) from Marlborough, Massachusetts.

Meanwhile Bennington in the southwestern corner of the state was Vermont's principal town during the generation after settlement. Burlington, with the University of Vermont (1793) and generations of lakeside commerce at the northern end of the state, was also a leading town in the early history of Vermont and attracted numerous furniture makers during the first half of the nineteenth century. While it is easy to list names that may later provide a clue, the craftsmen behind the vibrant furniture of western Vermont remain unidentified but were probably quite familiar with the market towns mentioned here.

CATALOGUE 56

Bureau, western Vermont, ca. 1810
Maple, birch, curly maple, and cherry veneers,
eastern white pine, brass
H. 42 ½ x W. 45 ½ x D. 19 ½ inches
Private Collection

CATALOGUE 56B

Detail, western Vermont bureau showing inlaid lozenge on dropped tablet.

Bureau, western Vermont, ca. 1815
Yellow birch, maple, butternut, birch, maple, and
mahogany veneers, eastern white pine, brass
H. 37 ⅝ x W. 45 x D. 20 ¼ inches
Private Collection

One Vermont Town's Furniture—Woodstock

Woodstock boasts Vermont's second-largest number of documented cabinetmakers, furniture makers, and chairmakers before 1855, with a total of 48, behind only Burlington, with 71 (followed by Bennington, 44, Brattleboro, 42, and Rutland, 43).[1] Shops and partnerships were established early in the town's history and were fluid, in both their physical and financial relationships. For example, Benjamin Metcalf formed a business with Ebenezer Richardson before 1820; after its dissolution,[2] Metcalf and Holland Burt joined forces from 1820 to 1822 (see Cat. 62 and Cat. 63).[3]

In 1823 Jacob Fisher and Thomas McLaughlin (see Cat. 65) announced they had taken the shop occupied by Benjamin Metcalf, who in 1824 began the manufacture of musical instruments with James Fisher, a painter. In 1825 Metcalf informed the public that he was about to leave town. He eventually died at St. Mark's Lighthouse near Tallahassee, Florida, in 1840.[4]

John Clark Dana and Israel Huntington worked briefly together from 1804 to 1805 (see Cat. 61), before Huntington moved to Vergennes after a fire destroyed his shop in 1808. Dana continued in the cabinetmaking trade prior to his untimely death in 1813 (see Cat. 58, Cat. 59, and Cat. 60). George Fisher (1820–96) trained in the shop of his father Jacob Fisher in Woodstock, where he worked as a cabinetmaker (see Cat. 66) in partnership with his brother, Isaac M. Fisher, from 1841 until after 1850.[5]

1. Charles A. Robinson, *Vermont Cabinetmakers & Chairmakers Before 1855: A Checklist* (Shelburne, VT: Shelburne Museum, 1994).
2. September 5, 1820, *Woodstock Observer*, Vol. I, Issue 35, 4.
3. Partnership dissolved April 16, 1822, *Woodstock Observer*, Vol. III, Issue 15, 4.
4. Henry Swan Dana, *History of Woodstock, Vermont 1761–1886* (Boston and New York: Houghton, Mifflin and Company, 1889) 160.
5. Robinson, *Checklist*, 53.

CATALOGUE 58
Sideboard, Woodstock, Vermont, 1804–13
Attributed to John Clark Dana (1779–1813) alone or in
partnership with Israel Huntington (b. 1781)
Mahogany and eastern pine with mahogany and birch
veneers and light and dark wood inlay
H. 40 ½ x W. 67 ½ x D. 25 ¼ inches
Woodstock Historical Society, 97.3.5

CATALOGUE 58 AND 59

Based on period advertisements and three surviving examples, "sash-cornered" sideboards seem to have been a specialty of John Dana.[1] Two of those sideboards are pictured here, both attributed to Dana. The third sideboard was built for Charles Dana (1781–1857), who in 1807 moved into the Dana House built by Nathaniel Smith at 26 Elm Street, now the home of the Woodstock Historical Society.

The first sideboard (see Cat. 58) is attributed to Dana as part of the furnishings of the Lightbourn House that he built at 29 Elm Street in 1808, and it is also in the collection of the Woodstock Historical Society.[2] It is similar to the Dana House sideboard (not pictured) in its layout and the use of oval veneers and maple cross-banding at the top and bottom of the case. The second sideboard illustrated here (see Cat. 59, in a private collection) can also be attributed to Dana for the unusual construction details that it shares with the other two pieces. These include double through-tenons that attach the horizontal members to the vertical drawer dividers. These enormous objects offered storage and desk functions, as indicated by the presence of vertical bottle drawers as well as the addition of a writing surface in the hinged top drawer of the Dana House example.

"Dana was accounted a good workman, and skilled in the art of making sash-cornered, serpentine and ogee sideboards, elliptic card-tables, etc. Furthermore, he was a quiet sort of man, disposed to live at peace with his neighbors, and averse to meddling in politics, but did get angry sometimes. Yet it is proper to observe, there may have been grounds and reasons with him for the occasional outbreak in this direction, which cannot be set forth here. . . . John C. Dana himself died in 1813 of lung fever."[3] Despite his short career, Dana's estate was large and included a "dwelling house and shop" valued at $1,500. The latter contained dozens of tools; four workbenches; a large quantity of mahogany, cherry, and basswood plank; numerous sets of furniture hardware; and several pieces of unfinished work, including a sideboard valued at $45.[4]

1. Robinson, *Checklist*, Dana & Huntington, 45.
2. For further information about the Swan, Gay, Dana, Marsh, and Marble families and their residence at 27 Elm Street and 37 Elm Street, see page 151.
2. Henry Swan Dana, 178, and Janet Houghton and Corwin Sharp, *Made in Woodstock: Furniture in the Collection of the Woodstock Historical Society* (Woodstock, VT: Woodstock Historical Society, 1997), 17.
3. Henry Swan Dana, 178.
4. John C. Dana inventory taken January 5, 1814, Hartford District Probate Records, 5:16-18, Hartford District Courthouse, Woodstock, Vt. See William N. Hosley, Jr., "Vermont Furniture, 1790–1830," *New England Furniture Essays in Memory of Benno M. Forman*, ed. Brock Jobe (Boston: Society for the Preservation of New England Antiquities, 1987), 249.

Sideboard, Woodstock, Vermont, 1804–13
Attributed to John Clark Dana (1779–1813)
Birch, mahogany and maple veneers, eastern white pine, brass
H. 40 x W. 70 ¼ x D. 24 ¼ inches
Private Collection

CATALOGUE 60
Kettle Stand, Woodstock, Vermont, 1805–13
Attributed to John Clark Dana (1779–1813)
Inscribed: Tape inside skirt "Dana Marsh"
Cherry, cherry and mahogany veneers, eastern white pine
H. 28 x W. 23 x D. 14 ¾ inches
Private Collection

CATALOGUE 60

The original purpose of this unusually shaped stand is unclear, although itinerant cabinetmaker Julius Barnard advertised in an 1805 Windsor, Vermont, paper that he had for sale "circular and octagon end tables."[1] Kettle or urn stands are rare survivals that also appear in several Portsmouth probate inventories in the 1780s, often in association with a tea table purchased by prominent merchants. These four-legged stands were just large enough to support the kettle or its neoclassical equivalent, the hot-water urn, used to brew and dilute tea.[2] Surviving examples are often fitted with an applied rim,[3] although this one is not. An oval ca. 1810 burl oak stand from Scotland, of nearly the same size and proportions (H. 26 ¾ x W. 22 x D. 16 ½ inches) as this Woodstock example, was offered for sale at the Olympia Fair in London in June 2013, which suggests a European prototype.[4]

This table was found at 37 Elm Street, Woodstock, in the left-hand ground floor room, where it was used as an end table. According to family tradition, it had been there since the house was built by Benjamin Swan in 1801, in a continuous chain of ownership which is corroborated by the very detailed family genealogy (see page 151) and summarized here. Benjamin Swan's neighbor, Charles Dana, residing at 26 Elm Street, married Mary Gay Swan, the niece of Benjamin's wife Lucy Gay. Charles was the elder brother of John Clark Dana, the furniture maker, living at nearby 29 Elm Street. These families were interrelated over several generations, and 37 Elm passed from the Swans to the Marshes to the Danas and eventually to the Marbles through marriage until the table was acquired by the current owner after 2011. The label on this stand confirms its provenance.

1. Ross Fox, "Julius Barnard (1769–after 1820) as Peripatetic Yankee Cabinetmaker," *Vermont History*, vol. 79 no.1 (Winter/Spring 2011), 9.
2. Brock Jobe, *Portsmouth Furniture: Masterworks from the New Hampshire Seacoast* (Boston: Society for the Preservation of New England Antiquities, 1993), figs. 50 and 51, heights are 27 inches and 30 inches respectively.
3. George Hepplewhite, *Cabinet-Maker and Upholsterer's Guide* (New York: Dover, 1959), plates 55 and 56.
4. Offered for sale by Alistair Drennan, email from owner, March 23, 2014.

CATALOGUE 61
Card Table, Woodstock, Vermont, ca. 1805
Cherry, maple and butternut (?) veneers, yellow birch, eastern white pine
H. 29 ½ x W. 34 x D. 16 ½ inches
Private Collection

CATALOGUE 61

This powerful card table boasts blocked front and sides with unusual square "turret" corners that seem to be vestigial supports for candlesticks, inspired by or derived from New York game tables with green baize covers.[1]

The visual focal point is the makers' careful placement of the tiger maple diamond inlaid on the blocked front. The bold cross-banding which is repeated on the edges of the hinged top, the bottom of the apron, and the cuffs of all four double tapered legs is also a distinguishing feature of the Dana sideboards (see Cat. 58 and Cat. 59); and the rectangular tablet strategically placed on the edges of the frame follows the same tradition as the Dana oval stand (see Cat. 60), which suggests that John Clark Dana may have made this table.

---

1. Oscar P. Fitzgerald, *Three Centuries of American Furniture* (New York: Gramercy Publishing Company, 1982), fig. IV-35.

CATALOGUE 62

This elegant sofa came from the house at 37 Elm Street in Woodstock, which was built by Benjamin Swan in 1801. The maker has concentrated his efforts on the arms and legs, which offer a familiar carving vocabulary. The combination of the incised cross-hatched pattern, somewhat uncomfortably placed on the top surface, with the acanthus leaf on the arm supports below (see Cat. 62B), relates to elements found on Otis Warren bureaus produced in nearby Pomfret,[1] as well as the Bugbee family drop-leaf table from Pomfret (see Zea Fig. 5, p. 20), while the vertical rope carvings are suggestive of the Woodstock stand from the same house (see Cat. 60).

1. Four-drawer chest, Pomfret, Vermont, signed "Otis Warren for Ledbetter, Norwich" in the same private collection.

CATALOGUE 62B
Detail, Benjamin Metcalf Sofa, showing deeply carved cross-hatched pattern on top of arm and acanthus leaf carving below.

CATALOGUE 62
Sofa, Woodstock, Vermont, ca, 1825
Attributed to Benjamin Metcalf (b. 1793–98, died 1840)
Mahogany, cherry, eastern white pine
H. 34 ½ x W. 76 ⅜ x D. 25 inches
Private Collection

CATALOGUE 63

In 1820 Benjamin Metcalf formed a partnership with Holland Burt (1790–1835) and advertised in the *Woodstock Observer* that they "have taken a shop in the upper part of the new brick building next door east of the Printing Office [in Woodstock], where they have on hand, or will furnish at short notice, Cabinet Furniture, in all its variety."[1] Surviving pieces include this Hepplewhite one-drawer stand at Shelburne Museum and a privately owned washstand derived from the "Bason Stand" in George Hepplewhite's 1794 design book.[2] Both pieces bear the same paper label: Benj. Metcalf & Co./Cabinet Makers/Woodstock, Vt. and date from 1820 to 1823, when Jacob Fisher & Thomas McLaughlin announced in the *Woodstock Observer* that they "have taken the shop recently occupied by Benj. Metcalf & Co."[3]

Metcalf's furniture label (see Cat. 63B) may have been produced by Metcalf himself. At some point in his career, Metcalf "invented and manufactured his celebrated printing press. . . . The entire process of printing was performed by the application of water or horse power to the principal wheel, with the exception of putting the sheets upon the tympan and taking them off, which was done by hand. The cost of one of these presses, made to work with one form only, was about $500, and it was found that an average workman in the use of it could easily turn off four hundred sheets an hour. Mr. Metcalf was successful in disposing of several specimens of his press, and it remained in use here and elsewhere for some time."[4]

In 1824 Metcalf and a new partner, James Fisher, "manufactured all kinds of musical instruments such as bass viols, flutes, violins, hautboy-reeds, etc. All the fine work was done by Metcalf, who was a superior mechanic, and the painting was done by Fisher. The partnership was dissolved in a short time, but Metcalf continued the manufacture of musical instruments to some extent as long as he remained in town. . . . In the course of a few years he removed from Woodstock to the Southern country, and died at St. Mark's Lighthouse, the 3d of July, 1840."[5] A fife made of boxwood, stamped "Metcalf" on the barrel, survives in the collection of Old Sturbridge Village.[6]

---

1. Robinson, *Checklist*, 78.
2. Hepplewhite, plate 83.
3. Robinson, *Checklist*, 78.
4. Henry Swan Dana, 160.
5. Henry Swan Dana, 160.
6. Old Sturbridge Village, Sturbridge, Massachusetts, acc. Number 10.17.96.

CATALOGUE 63

Stand, Woodstock, Vermont, 1820–23
Benjamin Metcalf (b. 1793–98, died 1840)
Cherry, basswood, and brass
H. 28 x W. 20 ¼ x D. 17 ¾ inches
Shelburne Museum, 1991–38

CATALOGUE 63B

Detail, Benjamin Metcalf Stand, showing paper label on bottom of
drawer: "BENJ. METCALF & CO./Cabinet Makers./Woodstock, Vt.

CATALOGUE 64
Stand, Woodstock, Vermont, 1825–35
Yellow birch, cherry, maple, eastern white pine, brass
H. 28 x W. 21 ¾ x D. 17 ⅞ inches
Private Collection

150

CATALOGUE 64

A number of subtle design elements contribute to the aesthetic success of this small stand. Constructed entirely of local woods without the addition of veneer or inlay, the stand shows the unidentified maker's shaping and lathe-work skills and commands the full attention of the viewer. The stamped eagle brasses form a focal point for the facade. The rounded case stiles, scalloped apron on front, back, and sides, and vigorous rope turnings that dominate the legs can be viewed from all angles and suggest the table was created for placement in the center of the room. It came from the Swan House, at 37 Elm Street, in Woodstock, built by Benjamin Swan in 1801.

THREE WOODSTOCK HOUSES AND THEIR OWNERS

Much of the furniture described and pictured in this chapter originated with members of an extended family and survived for many years in the homes for which these pieces were built: the 1807 "Dana House," at 26 Elm Street, the 1808 "Lightbourn House," at 29 Elm Street, and the 1801 "Swan House," at 37 Elm Street. The Woodstock Historical Society is now located at 26 Elm Street. The other two buildings are privately owned.

The men and women involved in the making and care of these homes and furnishings were interrelated by birth and marriage, as well as in business, and included members of the Swan, Gay, Dana, Marsh, and Marble families. Family first names are repeated across the generations, leading to potential confusion. Becky Talcott, a Woodstock historian and descendant of the families, provided valuable help in recounting their stories.[1]

The account begins with Ebenezer Gay, who married Mary Cotton Cushing in 1763. Among their five children were two daughters who married brothers: Mary married Timothy Swan (in 1784) and Lucy married Benjamin Swan (in 1804). Timothy and Mary Gay Swan had a daughter, also named Mary Gay Swan, who married Charles Dana (in 1808) and lived at 26 Elm Street. Benjamin and Lucy Gay Swan and their descendants lived at 37 Elm Street.

Charles and Mary Gay (Swan) Dana had eight children; the oldest son, Charles Jr., inherited the house at 26 Elm Street and the family dry-goods business. Charles Jr. and his wife Charitie (whom he married in 1848) had six children, five of whom survived, and some of them continued to live in the house until the last one passed away in 1942, when the house was acquired by the Woodstock Historical Society.

Benjamin and Lucy Gay Swan had four children; daughter Mary Frances Swan married Robert Southgate (in 1832) and daughter Lucy Gay Swan married Lyndon Marsh and lived at 37 Elm Street. The Southgates had a daughter Frances who married Edward Dana (in 1870); they were descended from the same great-grandparents, both on the mother's side. Mary Cotton Dana, daughter of Frances Southgate and Edward Dana, married Richard Merrill Marble (1916); their daughter, Mary Gay Marble Talcott, inherited 37 Elm Street in 1985. After her death in 2011, the house was sold out of the family.

1. Information provided by Becky Talcott from the collections of the Woodstock Historical Society, March 2015.

CATALOGUE 65

This stylish lady's worktable features figured mahogany, pressed glass drawer pulls, and saber legs, distinctive details that define Boston neoclassical furniture. It was among the early furnishings of the Light-bourn house, at 29 Elm Street, built by John Clark Dana in 1808.[1]

Jacob Fisher was the father of local cabinetmaker George Fisher (see Cat. 66). According to *The History of Woodstock, Vermont*, "the firm of Fisher and McLaughlin employed a great many hands and did more business than all other cabinet-shops round about put together. With some changes in the firm they continued business in the old shop [of Benjamin Metcalf from 1823] till 1835 when McLaughlin built, next above the old stand, the block that still goes by his name. . . . Two years after this he left Woodstock to take charge of the Clarendon House, Clarendon Springs, Vt."[2]

1. Houghton and Sharp, *Made in Woodstock*, 22.
2. Henry Swan Dana, 159-160.

Lady's Worktable, Woodstock, Vermont, 1829
Jacob Fisher (1791–1871) and Thomas McLaughlin (1800–71)
Inscription: Penciled on the lower drawer bottom:
"Fisher & McLaughlin/Woodstock/Oct. 28, 1829"
Mahogany, white pine, and basswood, with mahogany veneer,
pressed glass pulls
H. 27 ½ x W. 19 ¾ (with leaves down) x D. 20 ⅞ inches
Woodstock Historical Society, 97.3.9

CATALOGUE 66
Pier Mirror, Woodstock, Vermont, before 1841
George Fisher (1820–96)
Paper label: "GEORGE FISHER . . . Pleasant Street/WOODSTOCK, VT"
H. 31 ¼ x W. 22 ¼ (width at cornice) x (D. unrecorded)
Gilt eastern white pine and glass (original)
Private Collection

CATALOGUE 66

This classical pier mirror bears the label "GEORGE FISHER/MANUFACTUR-ER OF AND DEALER IN/Sofas, Mahogany Chairs and Tables,/AND EVERY VARIETY OF/HOUSEHOLD FURNITURE/Pleasant Street/WOODSTOCK, VT" (see Cat. 66B).

Born in Springfield, Vermont, George Fisher probably trained with his father, Jacob Fisher (1791–1871), a cabinetmaker who relocated before 1823 to Woodstock, where both men worked for the remainder of their lives.[1] George formed a partnership with his brother Isaac from 1841 until after 1850 under the name I. M. & G. Fisher and advertised in the *Vermont Standard*, April 29, 1853: "What Nots, and a good assortment of Mahogany, Black Walnut and Gilt Mouldings, for Frames . . . Looking Glasses/of all sizes, patterns and prices in Mahogany, Black Walnut and/Gilt Frames, which will be sold cheap. . . ."[2] One wonders whether Fisher applied his label to the looking glass as its retailer rather than its maker.

A classical card table in the Grecian taste also bearing his label in the collection of the Woodstock Historical Society[3] reveals George Fisher's awareness of changing styles and his embrace of current trends.

1. Robinson, Checklist, 53.
2. *Vermont Standard*, vol. 1, no. 1, April 29, 1853, in Houghton and Sharp, *Made in Woodstock*, 10.
3. Kenneth Joel Zogry, *The Best the Country Affords: Vermont Furniture, 1765–1850*, Philip Zea, ed. (Bennington, VT: The Bennington Museum, 1995), fig. 80.

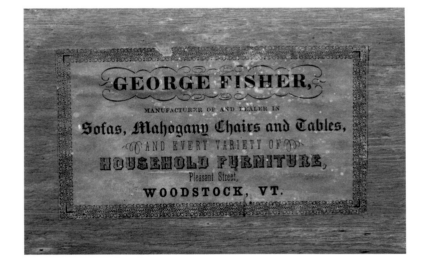

CATALOGUE 66B
Detail, George Fisher Pier Mirror, showing paper label with address and specialties of George Fisher.

The Best the Country Affords

CATALOGUE 67

Nathan Burnell, who was noted among cabinetmakers offering "the best the country affords,"[1] began his long career between 1811 and 1819 in Swanton.[2] His earliest documented piece of furniture is a bow-front bureau signed "N. Burnell/Swanton/May 13th 181(?)," made before his move to nearby Milton, where he remained for the rest of his life. Although it is unsigned, this Grecian-style table with central pedestal over scrolling base was found in the Milton house where he lived. The form—the top consisting of eleven, thirteen-inch long sides—and the materials, figured maple for all visible surfaces—make this table remarkable. The reason for this mathematically complicated design is unknown. This was clearly a specialty item, as Burnell's account book spanning over 40 years[3] lists only three center tables, two of which were sold for $20 (one to Joseph Clark, April 23, 1849, and one to Elisha Ashley, February 14, 1852) and one for $30 (to Sylvester Warn, April 13, 1849).

1. "Call at the fashionable Chair Factory a few rods east of Danville Green, or at the Cabinet Shop of Choate & Sias, in the village: where can be found Chairs, the best the country affords." William A. Hoyt, the *North Star,* Danville, Vermont, 1842.
2. Charles A. Robinson, *Vermont Cabinetmakers & Chairmakers Before 1855: A Checklist* (Shelburne, VT: Shelburne Museum, 1994), 39.
3. Covering the dates 1822–66, collection of Duane E. Merrill.

Center Table, Milton, Vermont, ca. 1850
Attributed to Nathan Burnell (1790–1866)
Bird's-eye maple and eastern white pine
H. 29 inches x W. 45 ½ inches diameter
Vermont Historical Society, 2011.22

CATALOGUE 68

Burnell's leather-bound ledger from 1822 to 1866 lists all customers alphabetically in an index at the front of the 217-page volume and provides a running account of each client's purchases and payment in goods or services ("contra") over the years they were buying. Surprisingly, no work tables or stands are recorded in the entire inventory. Burnell's output was prolific and included primarily "Beauro's"—a total of sixty-seven of them (butternut, maple, cherry, mahogany front, and birch) ranging in price from $15 to $28. Other high-value items were nine secretaries for $25 and three commodes for $40. Aside from the commodes, the single most expensive item in his entire account book was recorded on February 4, 1853, when he made a "Chamber Sett" for Daniel H. Onion (a regular customer from 1852 to 1862) for $35. Could this table be a part of that set? The table is classically inspired, with two "falls" supported by a central pillar over a square base with concave cutouts on turned feet, and features figured maple throughout. The surface materials relate this stand to Burnell's center table (see Cat. 67).

Two-Drawer Stand, Milton, Vermont, 1853
Nathan Burnell (1790–1866)
Inscription: Written in pencil on proper right side of bottom drawer
"Nathan Burnell, 1853"
Maple, yellow birch, maple veneer, basswood, eastern white pine
H. 28 ¾ x W. 16 ¼ (32 ¾ open) x D. 19 ⅞ inches
Private Collection

Stool, 1838
Mrs. Leonard, Pomfret, Vermont
Inscribed: Written in ink script on paper thumbtacked
underneath seat: "This 'ottomon' was/ made by Mrs.
Leonard/ in the town of Pomfret/ year of 1838"
Butternut, eastern white pine, and silk chenille fabric
H. 14 x W. 15 ¼ x D. 15 ⅛ inches
Private Collection

CATALOGUE 69

Footstools or crickets are rarely advertised by Vermont cabinetmakers and documented examples are rare. The legs on this "ottoman" appear professionally turned, suggesting that Mrs. Leonard installed the elegant fabric and advertised her proficiency with a needle with the accompanying inscription. The Leonard family were early inhabitants of Pomfret, arriving about 1791 or 1792, and they remained there for successive generations, until at least 1927.[1]

---

1. Henry Hobart Vail, *Pomfret Vermont* (Boston: Cockayne, 1930), vol. II, 529-33.

CATALOGUE 70
Bureau, 1830
Otis Warren (1807–67), Pomfret, Vermont
Inscription: Written in chalk under the bottom front rail:
"Warren/Pomfret VT Spl Comm/J Hill Randolph"
Maple and mahogany veneers, yellow birch, eastern white
pine, basswood, brass
H. 51 ½ x W. 43 x D. 21 inches
Private Collection

CATALOGUE 70

As stated in the chalk inscription, the maker recorded that this tour de force was a special commission for a J. Hill. The combination of a variety of highly figured woods, including flame birch and tiger and curly maple, with the vigorously turned and deeply carved columns (see Cat. 70B), concave gallery, and scrolling backsplash must have cost this customer in nearby Randolph a substantial amount.[1] One of this bureau's more intriguing design features is the central ebonized plinth, which is composed of four separate vertical pieces and is not drilled to receive a decorative finial.

Otis Warren was born in Pomfret and apprenticed in 1821 to an unidentified cabinetmaker in the neighboring town of Barnard. He must have been partial to the bureau form, as several related versions attributed to him appear in public and private collections.[2] His woodworking career was brief before he returned to Pomfret to study theology. In 1836 he relocated to Newfane, where he served as a clergyman until 1859.[3]

1. A search of United States Federal census records as well as town histories failed to identify a J. Hill in Randolph.
2. See Cat. 71, Otis Warren Bureau, and Kenneth Joel Zogry, *The Best the Country Affords*: *Vermont Furniture 1765–1850* (Bennington, VT: The Bennington Museum, 1995), fig. 74.
3. Henry Hobart Vail, *Pomfret Vermont*, vol. II, 383.

CATALOGUE 70B
Detail, Otis Warren Bureau, showing deeply carved and turned leg column.

CATALOGUE 71
Bureau, 1830
Attributed to Otis Warren (1807–67), Pomfret, Vermont
Mahogany and flame birch, eastern white pine, basswood, brass
H. 50 x W. 45 x D. 20 inches
Collection of J. Brooks Buxton

CATALOGUE 71

From top to bottom, this bureau is a testament to the cabinetmaker's mastery of both form and fashion. The scrolling splashboard punctuated with applied brass rosettes, stylish glove boxes, columns carved with vegetative elements, and careful wood selection throughout would have appealed to the most discriminating customer.

Most striking are the three-dimensional acorns protruding from the facade of the acanthus leaves surrounding the two drawers at the top of the case[1] (see Cat. 71B) as well as the exuberant deep rope turnings and bold, bulbous feet.

The deeply incised cross hatching found here above the turned feet appears to be a signature of Central Vermont work that is found on other Pomfret/Woodstock furniture (see Cat. 62 and Zea Fig. 5).[2]

1. See Cat. 70, Otis Warren Bureau.
2. There is also a bureau signed "Otis Warren for Ledbetter, Norwich" in a private collection.

CATALOGUE 71B
Detail, Otis Warren Bureau, showing carved acorn and acanthus leaves.

CATALOGUE 72
Bureau, Grafton, Vermont, ca. 1830
Samuel Walker (1791–1864)
Inscription: "Samuel Walker" written in pencil
on the bottom central drawer, top gallery
H. 52 ½ x W. 43 ⅞ x D. 20 inches
Cherry and basswood
Private Collection

CATALOGUE 72

In addition to the documentation provided by the penciled inscription, an owner recorded the provenance of this bureau, which descended in the family of Russell King (1801–74) and Ann Walker King Davison (b. 1805 or 1806) of Woodsville, New Hampshire, to Harold King Davison (b. 1893) and his wife Gladys.[1] Ann Walker was born in Rockingham, Vermont, and following her marriage there to Russell King in 1827 accompanied her husband to Woodsville in 1835.

The maker, born in Langdon, New Hampshire, to Samuel and Anna Walker in 1791,[2] migrated to Grafton, Vermont, in 1817 and, according to the town censuses, was engaged in agriculture there from 1820 to 1850.[3] The overall form of this bureau is similar to another signed bureau in the Grafton Historical Society[4] and shares the placement of leaf-carved panels at the top of the column, which here are flat, rather than three-dimensional. Unusual features on this bureau include the three flying fingers extending behind either side of the gallery and the turned, ebonized feet.

---

1. Following Gladys Davison's death in 1989, this bureau was sold at auction to another individual and then purchased by the current owner with this history.

2. New Hampshire Christenings 1714–1904.

3. Robinson, *Checklist*, 105. The relationship between Ann Walker King, the original owner, and Samuel Walker, the maker, has not been determined, although they could have been siblings. It is possible that Samuel Walker's parents moved from Langdon, New Hampshire, to Rockingham, Vermont (where they died), sometime between 1791 and the birth of his sister Ann in 1806. In 1817 Samuel Walker relocated to nearby Grafton, ten miles from Rockingham where Ann was married in 1827. Could this bureau have come into the Walker-King family at this time, perhaps as a wedding gift?

4. Zogry, *The Best the Country Affords*, fig. 75.

CATALOGUE 73B
Detail, Artemas Moses Chest of Drawers, showing stamped
brass back-plates and oval keyhole escutcheons.

CATALOGUE 73

Born in West Rutland, Artemas Moses is listed in 1815 as carrying on a trade as carpenter and joiner in Salisbury, Addison County,[1] although the finely crafted drawer dovetails used in the construction of this bureau appear far superior to his training. The vivid graining on the front and top of the piece—paint which may or may not have been executed by Moses—shows an appreciation for bookmatched mahogany, but in the interest of economy the sides are plain.

With his brother Orrin, Artemas Moses opened a shop in Middlebury on January 13, 1817, for the purpose of repairing clocks and watches. O & A, as the partnership was called, advertised that they carried a "very fine assortment of watch trimmings, silver table, tea, salt and cream spoons, gold beads, and bracelets."[2] The unusual stamped brass back-plates with zigzag design on this chest may be local work, although the oval keyhole escutcheons with beaded edge (see Cat. 73B) are found on other Vermont furniture.

1. John M. Weeks, *History of Salisbury Vermont* (Middlebury: A.H. Copeland, 1860), 126.
2. *Middlebury Standard* 1/15/1817 in Lillian Baker Carlisle, *Vermont Clock and Watchmakers, Silversmiths and Jewelers 1778–1878* (Burlington, VT: Stinehour Press, 1970), 211.

CATALOGUE 73
Chest of Drawers, Salisbury, Vermont, ca. 1825
Artemas Moses (1787– ca. 1825) Salisbury, Vermont
Inscribed in chalk inside backboard: "A. Moses Salisbury, VT."
Painted eastern white pine, paint, brass
H. 37 ½ x W. 38 ¼ x D. 18 inches
Private Collection

CATALOGUE 74

Sideboard, Saint Albans, 1840s

Attributed to William H. Livingston (1830–1916), Saint Albans, Vermont

Inscription: Handwritten in chalk on the inside of the case "B[u]y/Wm. H. Livingston" "Burlington, VT" and "April 28;" written in pencil on proper right back "repaired/by A.M. Woerner Scarsdale/Feb 7 1899"; and stamped in many places on interior wood, "G.P.Marsh"

Mahogany, mahogany veneer, and eastern white pine with gilding or bronze powder stenciling

H. 57 ¾ x W. 73 x D. 26 inches

Collection of the Vermont Historical Society, 2008.73

CATALOGUE 74

This recently discovered sideboard was acquired and conserved by the Vermont Historical Society and is the epitome of sophistication. It was purchased from a North Carolina dealer in 2008 with the history that it had most recently stood on the front porch of the Marsh house in Woodstock, Vermont, where George Perkins Marsh was born in 1801 and lived until 1825.[1] This exposure to the elements explains the structural damage and surface degradation it had sustained in later years. Its immense size and storage capacity (three drawers and three cupboards) indicate it was designed for use in a parlor or dining room, although, surprisingly, the sideboard is not equipped to hold bottles. The two large plinths could easily support ceramic or glass display pieces. The late pillar-and-scroll style, choice of select materials (flame-figured mahogany crotch veneer with gilt details), and masterful execution from the top pedestals to the carved hairy paw feet express the level of taste on the part of the original owner.

This is the only piece of furniture in this catalogue that displays the use of classically inspired border patterns executed with gold leaf and bronze powder applied either with stamps or stencils (see Cat. 74B). This type of embellishment was executed with great sophistication in the metropolitan centers of the eastern seaboard, particularly in New York City in the 1820s.[2]

During the 1840s and 1850s, William H. Livingston (1830–1916) worked in Saint Albans, Vermont, as a cabinetmaker in the household of his father, Horace Livingston (1798–1877), who advertised "an extensive assortment of the newest cabinet furniture" of the newest patterns including sideboards.[3]

After graduating from Dartmouth College, George Perkins Marsh (1808–82) embarked on his distinguished career in Burlington, as scholar, lawyer, congressman, and diplomat. He purchased a house on Pearl and Church Streets in the 1830s.[4] This remained his Vermont residence, following his 1839 marriage to his second wife Caroline Crane (1816–1901),[5] during his two Washington, DC, terms in Congress

(1843–49) and appointments overseas as Minister to the Ottoman Empire (1849–54) and later to the newly united Kingdom of Italy, where he spent the last twenty-one years of his life (1861–82). Clearly a man of taste and sophistication, Marsh was, however, plagued with perpetual penury[6] and periodic bankruptcy[7] throughout his career. It is highly questionable whether he chose to allocate his financial resources to acquiring such a flamboyant piece of furniture.

Based on the physical and biographical evidence, the following history of ownership is suggested. The sideboard might well have been a gift or presentation piece to Marsh from a wealthy political supporter as recognition for his Congressional service in the 1840s. The many "G.P. Marsh" stamps were most probably an effort to control the component parts throughout the production process in the originating workshop prior to the final assembly of the sideboard and shipment via rail from St. Albans to Burlington. Clearly a visible symbol of Marsh's prestige and accomplishments, the sideboard remained in his family. Following his death in 1882, Marsh's wife Caroline moved the sideboard to Larchmont, New York,[8] where it was later repaired by German craftsman Albert M. Woerner.[9]

1. David Lowenthal, *The Vermont Heritage of George Perkins Marsh, an Address before the Woodstock Historical Society* (Woodstock, VT: The Woodstock Historical Society, 1960), 2.

2. Cynthia Moyer, "Conservation Treatments for Border and Freehand Gilding and Bronze-Powder Stenciling and Freehand Bronze," *Gilded Wood Conservation and History*, edited by Deborah Bigelow, Elisabeth Cornu, Gregory Landrey, and Cornelis van Horne (Madison, CT: Sound View Press, 1991), 331–341.

3. Robinson, *Checklist*, 75.

4. David Lowenthal, *George Perkins Marsh, Versatile Vermonter* (New York: Columbia University Press, 1958), 35.

5. Jane & Will Curtis and Frank Lieberman. *The World of George Perkins Marsh, America's First Conservationist and Environmentalist* (Woodstock, VT: The Countryman Press, 1982), 29.

6. Curtis and Lieberman, 114.

7. Lowenthal, *The Vermont Heritage of George Perkins Marsh*, 2.

8. At some point following her husband's death and burial in Rome, Caroline Marsh relocated to Larchmont, New York, where she is listed in the 1900 Federal census.

9. 1930 Federal census, Albert Woerner, born 1854, living in Larchmont and working in the furniture industry.

CATALOGUE 74B
Detail, Sideboard attributed to William H. Livingston,
showing gilded details.

CATALOGUE 74C *(Overleaf)*
Detail, Sideboard, attributed to William H. Livingston,
showing carved hairy paw foot.

LENDERS TO THE EXHIBITION

Collection of J. Brooks Buxton

Fleming Museum of Art, University of Vermont

The Fowler Family

Collection of Norman and Mary Gronning

Historic Deerfield

Bernard and S. Dean Levy, Inc.

Duane Merrill

Ethan Merrill

Vermont Historical Society

Woodstock Historical Society

Several Private Collectors

PHOTOGRAPHY CREDITS

Photography by J. David Bohl

ADDITIONAL PHOTOGRAPHIC CREDITS

Courtesy Bennington Museum, photographer unknown: Fig. 2, p. 13, Fig. 3 p. 16, Fig 4, p. 19

Ken Burris, courtesy Bennington Museum: Cat. 37, Cat. 55, Cat. 58, Cat. 65

Ken Burris: Cat. 49

The Colonial Williamsburg Foundation: Cat. 27

Cottone Auctions, Geneseo, New York: Cat. 37B

Fleming Museum of Art, University of Vermont: Cat. 8

The Henry Ford: Cat. 15

Historic Deerfield: Fig. 5, p. 20, Cat. 20, Cat. 51

Hood Museum of Art, Dartmouth College: Fig. 2, p. 30

Bernard and S. Dean Levy, Inc.: Fig. 7, p. 23, Fig. 8, p. 24

New York State Museum: Fig. 9, p. 25; Cat. 48B, Cat. 48C

Old Sturbridge Village: Cat. 51

University of Vermont, Special Collections: Fig. 1, p. 10

SELECT BIBLIOGRAPHY

Carlisle, Lillian Baker. *Vermont Clock and Watchmakers, Silversmiths, and Jewelers, 1778–1878*. Burlington, VT: privately printed, 1970.

Dana, Henry Swan. *History of Woodstock, Vermont*. Boston: Houghton Mifflin Company, 1889.

Fox, Ross. "Julius Barnard (1769–after 1820) as Peripatetic Yankee Cabinet-maker." *Vermont History*, Vol. 79, No. 1 (Winter/Spring 2011), 1–25.

The Great River, Art & Society of the Connecticut Valley, 1635–1820. Gerald W. R. Ward and William N. Hosley, Jr., eds. Hartford, CT: Wadsworth Atheneum, 1985.

Hebb, Caroline. "A Distinctive Group of Early Vermont Painted Furniture." *The Magazine Antiques*, September, 1973 (Vol. CIV No. 3), 458–61.

Hebb, Caroline. "The South Shaftsbury, Vermont, Painted Wooden Chests." *Rural New England Furniture: People, Place, and Production*. The Dublin Seminar for New England Folklife Annual Proceedings 1998. Boston: Boston University, 1998.

Hepplewhite, George. *Cabinet-Maker and Upholsterer's Guide*. New York: Dover, 1959.

Hosley, William N., Jr. "Vermont Furniture 1790–1830." *New England Furniture: Essays in Memory of Benno Forman*, ed. Brock Jobe. Boston: Society for the Preservation of New England Antiquities, 1987.

Houghton, Janet, and Corwin Sharp. *Made in Woodstock, Furniture in the Collection of the Woodstock Historical Society*. Woodstock, VT: The Woodstock Historical Society, 1997.

Jobe, Brock. *Portsmouth Furniture: Masterworks from the New Hampshire Seacoast*. Boston: Society for the Preservation of New England Antiquities, 1992.

Montgomery, Charles F. *American Furniture: The Federal Period in the Henry Francis du Pont Winterthur Museum*. New York: Viking Press, 1966.

Mussey, Robert D., Jr. *The Furniture Masterworks of John & Thomas Seymour*. Salem, MA: Peabody Essex Museum.

Robinson, Charles A. *Vermont Cabinetmakers & Chairmakers before 1855: A Checklist*. Shelburne, VT: Shelburne Museum, 1994.

Zea, Philip. "Diversity and Regionalism in Rural New England Furniture." *American Furniture*. Milwaukee: The Chipstone Foundation 1995.

Zogry, Kenneth Joel. *The Best the Country Affords: Vermont Furniture 1765–1850*. Philip Zea, ed. Bennington, VT: The Bennington Museum, 1995.

CONTRIBUTORS

Jean M. Burks is curator emerita of Shelburne Museum.

Philip Zea is president of Historic Deerfield, Deerfield, Massachusetts.

Thomas Denenberg is director of Shelburne Museum.

Published in conjunction with the exhibition
Rich and Tasty: Vermont Furniture to 1850
Shelburne Museum
July 25–November 1, 2015

Rich and Tasty: Vermont Furniture to 1850 is made possible by the generous support of The Americana Foundation and J. Brooks Buxton.

Published by Shelburne Museum
P.O. Box 10
Shelburne, Vermont 05482
(802) 985-3346
www.shelburnemuseum.org

Distributed by
University Press of New England
1 Court Street, Suite 250, Lebanon, NH 03766

ISBN 978-0-939384-11-2

Production by Sandra M. Klimt, Klimt Studio, Inc.
Editing by Lucie G. Teegarden
Design by Margo Halverson, Alice Design Communication
Separations by Martin Senn
Printed by Verona Libri, Italy

Cover: Sofa (detail), ca. 1830, Middlebury, Vermont (Catalogue 39); attributed to Nahum Parker (1789–1876)
Back cover: Label, Benj. Metcalf & Co., Cabinet-Makers, Woodstock, Vermont (Catalogue 63)

Frontispiece: Worktable, ca. 1865; James Richardson (1794–1861), Poultney, Vermont (Catalogue 46). *Pages 2-3*: Detail, Bureau, Windsor, Vermont, 1810–15; attributed to Rufus Norton (1783–1818) (Catalogue 19).
Page 36: Detail, Lyman Briggs table, showing lyre pedestal (Catalogue 36B).
Pages 174–75: Detail, Middlebury Bureau, showing carved basket (Catalogue 35B).